Who put the Beef into Wellington?

To Vicky, Millie and Sam. I've written another one.

First published in Great Britain in 2012 by Kyle Books, an imprint of Octopus Publishing Group Ltd
Carmelite House
50 Victoria Embankment
London EC4Y 0DZ
www.octopusbooks.co.uk

An Hachette UK Company
www.hachette.co.uk

The authorized representative in the EEA is Hachette Ireland, 8 Castlecourt Centre, Dublin 15, D15 XTP3, Ireland (email: info@hbgi.ie)

This edition published in 2026 by Kyle Books

Copyright © Octopus Publishing Group Ltd 2012, 2026
Text copyright © James Winter 2012, 2026

Distributed in the US by
Hachette Book Group
1290 Avenue of the Americas,
4th and 5th Floors
New York, NY 10104

Distributed in Canada by
Canadian Manda Group
664 Annette St., Toronto,
Ontario, Canada M6S 2C8

All rights reserved. No part of this work may be reproduced or utilized in any form or by any means, electronic or mechanical, including photocopying, recording or by any information storage and retrieval system, without the prior written permission of the publisher. James Winter asserts the moral right to be identified as the author of this work.

ISBN: 978-1-8041-9370-9
eISBN: 978-1-8041-9371-6

A CIP catalogue record for this book is available from the British Library.

Printed and bound in Great Britain.

10 9 8 7 6 5 4 3 2 1

Publisher: Lucy Pessell
Senior Editor: Tim Leng
Assistant Editor: Samina Rahman
Designer: Isobel Platt
Production Controller: Sarah Parry

MIX
Paper | Supporting responsible forestry
FSC® C104740

This FSC® label means that materials used for the product have been responsibly sourced.

Who put the Beef into Wellington?

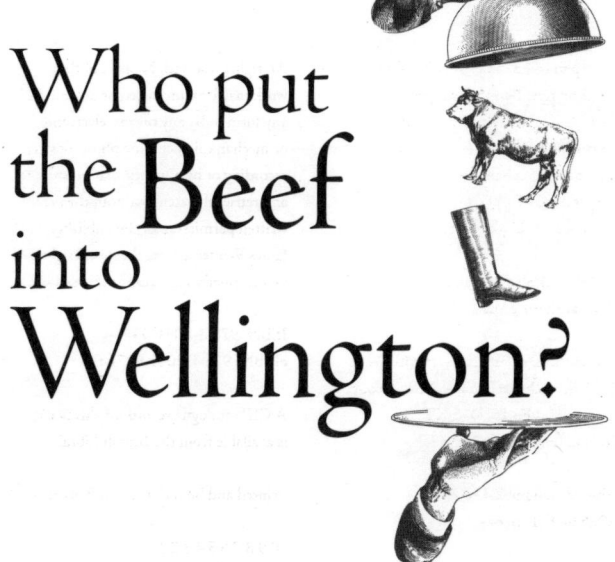

The Fascinating Stories Behind 50 Classic Recipes

James Winter

Contents

Foreword	6
Introduction	8
Caesar Salad	12
Waldorf Salad	18
Salad Olivier	24
Melba Toast	30
Eggs Benedict	36
Reuben Sandwich	42
Beef Carpaccio	48
Tournedos Rossini	54
Beef Stroganoff	60
Beef Wellington	66
Steak Diane	72
Veal Prince Orloff	78
Lamb Balti	84
Coronation Chicken	90
Chicken Marengo	96
Kung Pao Chicken	102
Chicken Kiev	108
Sole Véronique	114
Choron Sauce	120
Cod Mornay	126
Oysters Rockefeller	132
Lobster Thermidor	138
Omelette Arnold Bennett	144
Woolton Pie	150
Pommes Anna	156
Pizza Margherita	162

Tortellini	168
Pasta alla Norma	174
Pavlova	180
Apple Charlotte	186
Bananas Foster	192
Baked Alaska	198
Crêpes Suzette	204
Peach Melba	210
Tarte Tatin	216
Battenberg Cake	222
Opera Cake	228
Madeleines	234
Lamington	240
Garibaldi biscuits	246
And to Drink ...	252
Bellini	253
Cosmopolitan	256
Margarita	259
Martini	262
Piña Colada	265
Mint Julep	268
Negroni	271
Sidecar	274
Ramos Gin Fizz	277
Tom Collins	280
Conversion chart	283
Index	284
Acknowledgements	288

Foreword

To fully understand food you have to work with it and not just eat it, you have to live it and breathe it. Some choose to spend their days reading books to learn more, others like myself, have chosen to work behind the stoves. James Winter, as you will see from reading further into this book, has gained it a third way. Working around chefs, foodies and journalists, but above all travelling and tasting the food the world has to offer. I have known James for over 20 years and his knowledge of food is second to none. I should know, I used it all the time on *Saturday Kitchen*. This has given him a real insight into the subject of food and with so many young chefs nowadays reaching for the liquid nitrogen and espuma guns this book is all about the best of food. I learnt quickly as a chef that to go forward and write new dishes you have to always look back, there is very little that hasn't been done before. Such recipes have been perfected and made by cooks for years and are slowly starting to creep back onto chefs' menus.

What's as important as the recipes, are the stories behind how the dishes were first made and how they acquired the names we all know and love today. Waldorf Salad is as classic as Eggs Benedict and in this book you will learn why they both have stood the test of time – you would have to find several books to learn more about either. This book and James's take on the dishes takes you on a culinary journey of fascinating facts and tales about who invented what and why.

I hope this book will inspire you as you learn more about great chefs like Marie-Antoine Carême, Auguste Escoffier and Adolphe Duglèré and, above all else, get into the kitchen to try the recipes from these legends. These men were the Robert Stephenson, Isambard Kingdom Brunel and James Watt of the food world, the like of which has never been seen since. Their hard work and inventive styles are still the backbone of cooking today and this book is full of fascinating tales from time in the kitchen.

So if you really want to know just 'Who put the beef in the Wellington?', then read on, as there is no one better to tell you than James Winter.

— JAMES MARTIN

Introduction

'The discovery of a new dish confers more happiness on humanity than the discovery of a new star.'

— JEAN ANTHELME BRILLAT-SAVARIN

These are big, bold words but Brillat-Savarin was a big, bold man. Very few thought about food as much as he did and very few ate as many gastronomic delights. He devoted his life to exploring the human relationship with food and he loved every minute of it. New dishes excited him and chefs' creative exertions fascinated him. His great work *The Physiology of Taste* was published in 1825 and it is still relevant today with its focus on good taste and obesity. He was an important figure of his time and is recognized as the very first gourmet.

I am not a gourmet, more of an enthusiast or keen observer. I adore stories and the journeys that people and recipes have taken to end up how or where they are today. So certain dishes have always fascinated me, they are often named after a person or an event or even a location. You would think then when a recipe is labelled in such a way as to give you a first clue that the rest would fall into place but the truth is a little different. Tracing the origins and the first discovery of new dishes is surprisingly tricky. Despite all his passion and power for the subject, Brillat-Savarin never devoted much time to how or why new dishes were created. It seems he was not alone in not documenting the wonders that he found either. The idea behind this book was to shed just a glimmer of light upon the culinary magic of some of the great chefs and cooks of our food past. For a long time recipes were rarely written down and when they were there was no guarantee they were scribed by the inventor of the dish. Sometimes several people published the same recipe around the same time with no credit given to one or another to point to its origin. Food is always better when it's shared and the same goes for recipes; they also spread rapidly from chef to chef and country to country. For this reason chefs often attempt to hide the exact details of a dish to protect it from prying eyes and so prolong their secret and thus be able to charge their diners for the exclusivity of their recipes.

When a chef makes something new they have no comprehension of how seismic the creation is. It may be forgotten in a night or it may live on at other dinner tables or on other menus long after the chef has gone. It's also hard to judge which dishes will stand the test of time. One could argue that some recipes such as meringue or béchamel sauce are so useful and versatile that it was inevitable that they should survive and prosper but others are a singular piece of wonderment like a Peach Melba or an Omelette Arnold Bennett. There is no logical reason why they should still remain popular or relevant. So the second task set among these pages was to pick dishes that were larger than their component parts, which stood tall among an overpopulated culinary world. There are 50 recipes here, each with a story, each with twists and turns and each with a delicious ending, literally!

Information about their origins is surprisingly hard to come by. The recipes are commonplace but the people who invented them are lost in the mists of time. Shreds of anecdotal evidence lie here and there but all in all it is all rather vague. I have tried to weave these threads together into some kind of sense using the best information I could find. But like all good stories there are many variations and interpretations and so I am sure some may disagree with my version of events and to those people I offer an invitation to share their ideas, preferably over a glass of wine, and set me straight.

The process of creation takes on many forms, it can be quick and explosive or long and painful or anywhere in between. Chefs are like any other artist; their tools are fruit, meats, vegetables and fish, the same ingredients we can all purchase from any local store. The difference is in how we put these things together, like a jigsaw puzzle whose pieces can be put together in a million different ways but only a real master can see the true picture. The difference between say a painter and a chef is in the end product. An artist who works with oils and canvas can stand back and admire his creation; it won't dissolve or fade or, more importantly, be eaten. It often has the painter's name and the date he finished the work written handily on the front and it hangs on a gallery wall for others to love and enjoy. If properly looked after it will last for hundreds of years and can accrue great value. For a chef the end product has a very different life. It is a plate of food after all; often a very pretty and beautiful plate of lovely colourful things, but ultimately it has one function. Its lifespan is short and its aim is to excite our taste buds and satisfy our stomachs. It provides an instant hit and an empty plate; once it has gone it has gone forever. A recipe is like a photograph, it gives us a limited recording of the process. It is a starting point, a template if you will. All the recipes in this book are there to start you off. They are the way I like to cook the dishes and as close to the way they first began as is practical. You can, of course, adapt them, change them, and improve them. It is in your power.

The food world is full of colourful characters, anyone who has sat in a restaurant in the middle of the afternoon or wandered through the many great food markets of the world can see the incredible diversity of passionate people either buying or selling food. I love these people, they are the lifeblood of our food culture and I want to introduce you to some of the names from our culinary past. Each of the dishes included here is like a theatrical event, a story of powerful creative forces coming together to make something new. You will read about chefs such as Carême, Escoffier, Dubois and Dugléré; there are queens of Italy and Roman goddesses, Russian princes and French emperors. I have tried to throw just a little light on their achievements and to put into context their contribution to our colourful food history. They were all great men and women and I hope that by putting a spotlight on their work I can keep their memory burning bright and see the journey that cookery has taken in the last few hundred years thanks to their help.

These days the shelves of book shops are awash with cookery titles and many newspapers and magazines carry a recipe in every edition, but go back one hundred years and this was certainly not the case. The 50 recipes in this book are classics and have stood the test of time. They have been passed on, at first, by reputation from chef to chef and then later in a few seminal cookbooks and now, in modern times, have been repeated over and over by new chefs and cooks all over the world. They're all things I love to cook and, more importantly, love to eat. They have helped me make new friends and led to some great evenings swapping stories and food experiences. I just hope the tales in this book help you do the same, dip in and out, read it as and when you wish and use the information to spread a little tasty joy to people. Get hungry, get stuck in and get cooking.

Caesar Salad

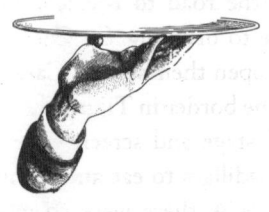

It has to be said that, for most of us, the word 'salad' does not conjure up feelings of enormous excitement. It's a culinary option associated with diet and denial; the dish on the menu you choose when you want something else but know you shouldn't. However, put the name Caesar in front of it and you instantly have an image of Saturday night indulgence; of rich dressing and salty umami goodness that turn a plain old lettuce leaf into a vessel for the most famous salad ingredients in the world.

Caesar Salad is so luxurious that it may surprise you to learn that its origins lie in 1920s America, where Prohibition was in full force. The ban on alcohol was introduced in 1920 with the aim of reducing political and social corruption and domestic violence. What actually happened was that organized gangs began producing alcohol on a large scale to supply to their illegal drinking dens or speakeasies. Not surprisingly, restaurateurs who kept on the right side of the law struggled with the downturn in business that Prohibition had brought with it.

One of these law-abiding citizens was Caesar Cardini who, from his restaurant in San Diego, California, looked enviously down the road to Mexico, where there was a different attitude to drinking. So Caesar and his brother Alex decided to open their second Caesar's Italian restaurant just across the border in Tijuana.

Soon stars of stage and screen were rushing down in their drop-top Cadillacs to eat and drink. The story goes that, on 4 July 1924, there were so many of them that food supplies began to run low. There was little in the fridge except lettuce, and with so much liquor flowing Caesar needed something to fill hungry stomachs. A bit of a showman himself, he struck upon the idea of preparing a salad at the table, in front of his guests: 'Let them think they are having our speciality,' he cried. And so it began.

I don't need to tell you that it was a huge hit. Caesar Salad was the food sensation of the 1920s, with everyone from Clark Gable to W C Fields making the pilgrimage to Tijuana to eat it. 'Going for a Caesar' became the hip holiday for the hippest of crowds.

Hippest of the hip in the 1930s was the socialite Wallis Simpson, future Duchess of Windsor. She fell for Caesar Salad on one of her many trips to Tijuana and made sure all her important friends from Baron Rothschild to Yves Saint Laurent tried it. She also took the recipe to Europe and demanded that the chefs in many of the continent's top restaurants prepare it to her instruction. Legend has it that Wallis was the first to cut the lettuce into delicate, bite-sized pieces so that it could be eaten with fingers as a canapé.

In 1938 the Cardinis moved to Los Angeles, where Caesar opened a gourmet food store and, working with his daughter Rosa, began to bottle and sell his dressing across America. One version of the story describes his early patrons arriving with empty wine bottles to be filled with dressing; another says that their enterprise started with bottling and labelling at home, then selling from the back of the family station wagon at the local farmers' market.

Meanwhile, the dish took on a life of its own; people began to add chicken or fish to the salad to bulk it up, while at a later restaurant, Alex Cardini launched a variation with whole anchovies on top, which he called an Aviator Salad. (Caesar himself disapproved of this; he believed the subtlety of the salad would be overwhelmed by the oily fish. The now familiar fishy tang in the dressing comes from the Worcestershire sauce alone.)

A further lease of life came when the American chef Julia Child demonstrated the recipe on TV in the 1970s. She had been taken to Caesar's as a child in the 1920s and later wrote that her parents were 'so excited when big jolly Caesar himself came to the table to make the salad… it was dramatic: I remember…how he tossed the leaves so that it looked like a wave turning over.' When she became a television chef she contacted Rosa for the authentic recipe – with no anchovies.

Caesar Salad remains a great dish to throw into your dinner parties, especially if you do it Cardini-style at the table. Or you can have it alone with a good film and a glass of crisp Sauvignon – or tequila, if you like your showbiz lifestyle. I dare you not to love it. Show me a person who doesn't like a Caesar Salad and I'll show you my hen's teeth risotto!

 # Caesar Salad

Crunchy fresh lettuce is the key to this dish, wash it well and dry it thoroughly before use. Feel free to add chicken to this dish if you want to make it more substantial but for parties keep it simple and light.

Serves 4

- 6 tablespoons olive oil, plus a little extra for frying
- 1 large garlic clove
- 1 large free-range egg
- 1 tablespoon lemon juice
- 2 teaspoons Worcestershire sauce
- freshly ground black pepper
- 2 thick slices of white bread, crusts removed, cubed
- 1 Romaine lettuce, washed and the leaves carefully removed, leaving whole and long
- 25g Parmesan cheese, coarsely grated

- Pour the oil into a saucepan and add the garlic. Gently warm the oil over a low heat. You are not trying to fry the garlic but get the oil to blood temperature. Remove from the heat and set aside for about 30 minutes.

- Put the egg into a saucepan of cold water and bring to the boil. Boil for 1 minute and then plunge the egg into cold water to stop the cooking process. Crack the egg into a food processor and add the garlic and olive oil, lemon juice and Worcestershire sauce. Process well and season with pepper to taste.

- Fry the bread cubes in a little olive oil until golden and crispy, then set aside to drain on kitchen paper.

- To serve, place the Romaine lettuce in a bowl. Pour over the dressing and add the croutons and Parmesan. Coat the leaves in the dressing, then serve by placing the leaves with their thin edge out in a circle and put the salad in the middle of the table for people to eat with their fingers.

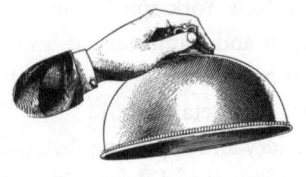

Waldorf Salad

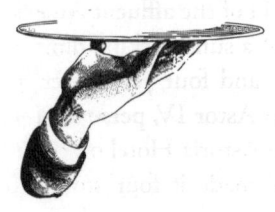

There's no doubt that New York is one of the most incredible cities in the world, full of ruthless ambition and endless excitement. If you want it and you can pay for it, then you can have it. There is no dish that better typifies the New York spirit than the Waldorf Salad. Cole Porter knew it and immortalized it in his song 'You're the Top': his lyrics put the salad on a par with the *Mona Lisa*, the Tower of Pisa and Greta Garbo's salary. It's just a mixture of mayonnaise, celery and apple on a bed of lettuce, but it is a perfect balance of sweet and sharp with soft and bitter. The Waldorf is a salad that is definitely bad for you but makes you feel good, just like New York.

The Waldorf=Astoria Hotel was born out of conflict. The 13-storey Waldorf half was built in 1893 by the richest man in America, William Waldorf Astor, on the site of his former residence. It also happened to be next door to his aunt, the wonderfully named Caroline Webster Schermerhorn Astor, with whom he had been feuding for some time: Caroline believed that she should have sole use of the name 'Mrs Astor', while William maintained that his wife was entitled to use it too. This was an important matter in the world of the affluent American socialite.

The erection of a sun-blocking building did nothing to appease Caroline and four years later her son, William's cousin John Jacob Astor IV, persuaded her to move away. He then built the Astoria Hotel on the adjoining block to the Waldorf, and made it four storeys higher. Although originally separate, the two were soon connected by some clever architecture and the now famous double-hyphen. This both emphasized the equality between the two buildings and visually represented the small alleyway that separated them on the ground.

The Waldorf and later the Waldorf=Astoria changed the way hotels function. No longer were they merely for transient people looking for somewhere to rest their heads; now they would be magnets for the rich and powerful who wanted to enjoy themselves. The Waldorf=Astoria's glamorous bars and sophisticated restaurants were soon full of New York's A-listers, most with the surname Astor or Vanderbilt or, failing that, invited by them. The hotel was also the last word in service and attention to detail. From the day the Waldorf opened its doors it provided room service – the first hotel to do so. Imagine, if you had never heard of the idea before, the sheer joy of being able to eat food at any hour of the night without leaving your room! It also contained within its walls an inner sanctum, a hotel within a hotel. These Waldorf Towers were a highly exclusive collection of rooms which played host to some of the most powerful and famous people in America. Residents ranged from the inventor Nikola Tesla through to the notorious New York gangster Bugsy Siegel.

The driving force behind many of these innovations and the creator of the salad that bears part of the hotel's name was the maître d', Oscar Tschirky. Oscar was on board from the opening of the Waldorf and in charge of the planning and the pre-opening parties. In those days the maître d' had many culinary jobs to do, including boning fish tableside and preparing fresh salads, and the flamboyant Oscar knew that the hotel needed some signature dishes to make it stand out. He saw the chance to put together a few of his favourite things, mayonnaise, apple and celery, and he served them on small lettuce leaves so they looked glamorous and tasty. He unleashed his salad on 1,500 New York socialites, press and celebrities just a week before the official opening and overnight it became the talk of the town. It has never left the hotel menu since – and today if you order it from room service it contains truffles!

Oscar was a passionate foodie and an avid collector of menus and recipes. In 1896 he published his own cookbook, simply entitled *The Cookbook*. Its success enabled people across the country – and the world – to replicate the salad that had swept New York.

Oscar's original version didn't contain walnuts; that change may have been the brainchild of George Rector, a successful restaurateur in the 1920s at an eatery named after himself. He featured a walnut-including version in his *Rector Cook Book* in 1928. These days you may see anything from grapefruit to cauliflower included in a Waldorf Salad – my version, like many others, includes grapes – but Oscar Tschirsky's original dish still has the power to conjure up an image of high-class hotel living.

 # Waldorf Salad

'Peel two raw apples and cut them into small pieces, say about half an inch square, also cut some celery the same way, and mix it with the apple. Be very careful not to let any seeds of the apples be mixed with it. The salad must be dressed with a good mayonnaise.'

— THE ORIGINAL RECIPE, FROM *THE COOKBOOK* BY OSCAR OF THE WALDORF, 1896

Serves 4

- 4 medium-sized celery sticks, chopped into approx. 1cm pieces
- 50g walnut halves, roughly chopped
- 2 teaspoons freshly chopped chervil
- 2 Granny Smith apples, peeled and diced into 1cm pieces (make sure no pips sneak in as they are very bitter indeed)
- freshly ground black pepper
- a handful of crunchy lettuce leaves
- 85g seedless black or white grapes, halved

For the dressing
- 1 garlic clove
- ½ teaspoon sea salt
- 3 tablespoons mayonnaise
- 1 heaped dessertspoon natural yogurt

- Put the chopped celery in a bowl with the walnuts.

- To make the dressing, crush the garlic in a pestle and mortar with the sea salt. Mix the mayonnaise and the yogurt together and add to the mortar and mix. Add this to the celery and walnuts.

- Now add the chopped chervil to the dressing along with the apple. Toss everything together, ensuring that the dressing has coated all the ingredients and season with pepper. Serve on the lettuce leaves and garnish with the grapes.

Salad Olivier

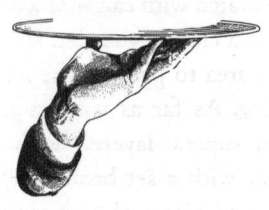

If there is one dish that unites a much-divided Eastern Europe it is this rich but luxurious mixture of game and crayfish lightened with a piquant mayonnaise. It is the national dish in at least four countries including Bulgaria, Serbia and North Macedonia; most places east of Poland serve it at New Year and at many other celebrations. It makes a stunning centrepiece to any buffet and the story of its creation and subsequent rise to culinary classic status might have come straight out of a Russian spy novel.

By 1860 the Russian dining classes had been in love with all things French for some time. French chefs were employed in any aristocratic household worth its salt. However, life in Russia is much colder than in France and involves a lot more vodka, so flavours have to be big and bold. One chef who understood this was Belgian-born Lucien Olivier, who in 1864 opened a restaurant called the Hermitage in Moscow.

The Hermitage served Russian dishes with a classical French influence. Sauces were refined and rich, but the gamey meats and dried fish were local and very Russian. As a way to use up ingredients, Olivier invented a salad but, as the Hermitage was a fine-dining restaurant, it had to be decadent and decorated with caviar as a final flourish.

The recipe was a closely guarded secret: Olivier would retire to his own area to prepare the *mise en place* and to make the dressing. As far as we can tell it consisted of black caviar and capers, layered with steamed chicken and held together with a set broth made from the bird's carcass. Crayfish and pieces of beef tongue were arranged around the edges of the dish and it was dressed with an emulsion of olive oil, egg yolks, French vinegar, mustard and spices. A potato skin filled with gherkins and chopped boiled egg decorated the centre of the dish.

The restaurant and the dish were a huge success. For the first time Moscow had an eatery as fine as anything in Paris. But other chefs regarded Olivier's good fortune with envious eyes and even among his own employees there were those willing to stab him in the back. The waiting staff were not given wages but relied purely on tips; if they were to get their hands on the golden goose of a recipe they could make a pretty penny. So when on one busy night around 1880 Olivier was called away from his prep to deal with a culinary emergency, a sous chef by the name of Ivan Ivanov saw his chance, dashed into the boss's work area and rapidly made a note of everything he could see.

Ivanov immediately left the Hermitage and got a job at a restaurant called Moskva, where he served something he called 'Capital Salad'. Olivier's recipe was finally out there. Despite critics damning it as inferior, Ivanov was able to get it published and earn himself some money. Very soon variations were appearing in every restaurant in Russia. Olivier himself died in 1883 and his family left the country after the 1905 revolution, leaving other chefs free to sell their versions of the dish as Salad Olivier. In a final twist to the story of this secretive man, his tomb was discovered only in 2008, hidden away in the German cemetery in Moscow. Rumour has it that his recipe book was buried alongside him.

Changing economic conditions meant that food had to change too. Caviar and game were not on most people's menus and Salad Olivier became a catch-all name for most Russian salads. When many Russians left the country in 1917 they set about redefining the salad's ingredients in their new homes: an Iranian version includes chicken, gherkins and carrots, a Turkish one sliced cucumber pickles and a Polish one potatoes, carrots, onions, dill pickles and apples but no meat.

After the Second World War Russian communities all over the globe began to look to the dishes of their past to use at times of celebration and Salad Olivier became the centrepiece to many. These days it is as important to New Year as the turkey is to Thanksgiving in the United States. In Britain memories of Russian Salad were scarred a little by the tinned variety in the 1970s, but my advice is to forget what the school dinner ladies called Russian Salad, get stuck in to this rich combination of flavours and transport yourself back to nineteenth-century Moscow. You can include herring roe instead of the caviar if you really want to go the full nine yards – and why wouldn't you? Overleaf is my version of the salad, which is much more accessible than Olivier's original, but no less delicious.

Salad Olivier

Using chicken breasts on the bone with the skin on helps keep the moisture in the meat and gives the dish a fuller flavour. It really needs the sharpness of the mustard and cornichons to cut through all the mayonnaise so try to keep the flavours balanced and taste as you go to stop the salad becoming too heavy.

Serves 4–6

- 2 large chicken breasts, on the bone with the skin on
- 1 bay leaf
- 6 peppercorns
- 1 onion, chopped into chunks
- 1 potato
- 125g full-fat mayonnaise
- 75g natural yogurt
- 2 teaspoons Dijon mustard
- juice of 1 lime
- 1 tablespoon white wine vinegar
- a handful of finely chopped tarragon
- 2 tablespoons olive oil (Spanish if you can get it)
- 10–12 cornichons
- a handful of finely chopped parsley
- 2 hard-boiled eggs
- 100g small prawns, cooked
- Sevruga caviar, to taste
- 12 white endive leaves

- Poach the chicken in about 200ml water along with the bay leaf, peppercorns and onion for about 40 minutes until the chicken is very soft. Leave it to cool in the water. Remove the skin and pull the meat from the bone. Chop the meat into small cubes.

- Meanwhile, boil the potato in a saucepan of water until just tender, ensuring that it does not go completely soft. Leave it to cool and chop into cubes.

- Mix together the mayonnaise, yogurt, mustard and lime juice. Add the vinegar little by little, checking the flavour to stop it becoming overpowering. Add the tarragon and the oil and mix well.

- Chop the cornichons into very small pieces and add them to the mayonnaise along with the chicken, potato and the parsley. Mix well – it's fine if the potato breaks up a little. If the mixture seems a bit thick then add a little of the poaching liquid from the chicken to loosen it up.

- Finally chop the eggs and fold through the mixture along with the prawns. Tip the mixture into a shallow bowl, top with the caviar and put the endive leaves around the edge so people can eat from the leaf if they wish.

Melba Toast

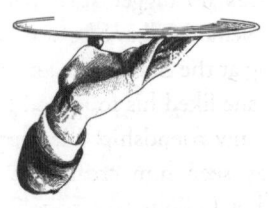

Often the simplest things in life are the work of the greatest minds: it takes immense talent and bravado to strip back the creative process and present a product without elaborate garnishes, knowing that it is perfect for the occasion. Nowhere is that truer than of Melba Toast. It's not just toast, it's perfect toast! Its curly, crunchy brittleness is the ideal foil for anything from a scoop of cream cheese to a rich, brandy-fuelled pâté. Its seductive curve is always an exciting indicator of tasty things to come. If someone has made the effort to make Melba Toast as a starter, what follows will surely be a delight.

Melba Toast was created just over a century ago, in 1897, when the great Auguste Escoffier was at the height of his powers at the Savoy Hotel in London. The food he served to the great and good was hailed as the best in the world. The Savoy was the hotel of choice for royalty, business tycoons and, most memorably, celebrities. Celebrity culture may have reached its zenith in our own century, but it has always existed. As soon as humans invented shows, show business was the natural by-product. It catapulted its stars into the public eye. Back in 1897, for the culture-rich Londoner, there was no bigger star than the Australian songstress Dame Nellie Melba. She was often in England and enjoyed staying at the Savoy. She and Escoffier became well acquainted – she liked his food and he liked his food, a perfect basis for any friendship. Her appreciation of his talents had already seen him create the stunning Peach Melba dessert in her honour (see page 210) and she was always able to turn to the great chef to find something to suit her tastes and needs.

On this particular trip, though, Nellie was feeling unwell. She retired to her room, sending down a request to the kitchen for some plain toast, something dry and without much flavour. Now asking one of the greatest chefs in the world to make you some toast is akin to asking Caravaggio to give your bedroom walls a lick of paint – the chances are he is going to over-deliver.

One can only imagine the scene in the kitchen. Escoffier placing the slices of bread under his grill and watching as their outsides turn slowly golden. Then removing them and examining them, deciding they are not crispy enough. A sharp blade slices the toast down the middle; the now pale side is put back under the flame. The great man smiles a little as the corners begin to curl slightly, their texture perfect for his operatic guest's weary digestive system. Escoffier sent the toast up. It never came back. It became a staple of Nellie's diet during her recuperation and on future visits.

There is, of course, an alternative version which has the toast being made by a bungling young waiter. It drew gasps of horror from the hotel owner, César Ritz, but before he could apologize the Dame had declared, 'I have never eaten such lovely toast.' Melba Toast made it all the way on to the Savoy Grill menu, served with pâtés and cheese, and remained there for over a hundred years.

To understand how these humble crisp breads took on a life beyond London's West End, you need to look to our increasing obsession with body shape and diet. In the 1920s the Mayo medical clinic in Rochester, Minnesota, well known for its innovative techniques, was asked by the actress Ethel Barrymore to help her lose weight. Barrymore was one of the great stars of the silent movie era, but she was now in her forties and she wanted to remain a star. The 18-day diet the Mayo created for her relied heavily on Melba's little crispy toasts. Celebrity culture in 1920s America was much more evolved than it had been in Britain in the 1890s and American housewives spent long days under the hairdryer devouring every details of the lives of the rich and famous. Word of this 'miracle toast' soon spread and suddenly it was everywhere, as satisfying as toast but with half the calories.

It didn't take long for a couple of successful bakers, Harry and Sophie Cubbison, to work out how to mass-produce the toast, package it and get it on to the supermarket shelves. Their company, Mrs Cubbison's Foods, still exists today, largely thanks to Melba Toast and its use in stuffing and other coatings.

Incidentally, Ethel Barrymore went on to enjoy a long and productive career in the talking-picture business, but I leave it to you to decide if Melba Toast was responsible.

 # Melba Toast

Melba Toast is one of those dishes that is brilliantly ingenious to make. It is so simple but serve it to friends with rustic duck rillettes or a smooth chicken liver pâté and they are going to be impressed.

Makes 2

- 1 slice of bread

- Place the slice of bread under the grill and toast for a couple of minutes until lightly golden on both sides.

- Remove from the grill and splice the slice with a sharp knife and return to the grill, uncooked side up. Watch carefully and remove when golden.

- Serve with the pâté of your choice.

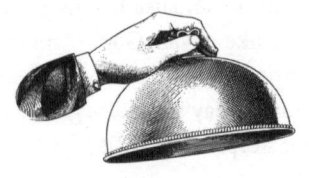

Eggs Benedict

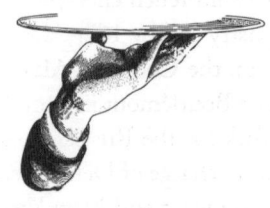

There is something utterly desirable about a dish that can work just as well as a breakfast, a lunch or a late-night snack. The combination of soft, rich egg and salty-sweet ham sitting on a crisp, forgiving muffin with a lick of silky smooth hollandaise hanging over it is the work of a master, much like a Van Gogh sunflower or a Renoir umbrella. It is fitting that the story of a dish that can be enjoyed at any time of day should begin in the 24-hour city, the city that never sleeps: New York.

The year was 1890-something; Manhattan was a thriving, bustling island. Wall Street was emerging as the smart road to work on. Guys called John D Rockefeller and J P Morgan had set up shop and people were trading shares daily, while a man named Charles Dow (later to hook up with Edward Davis Jones and become synonymous with the New York Stock Exchange) kept track of the dozen or so stocks in his reports. This was a time of furious creation.

Just two blocks south from Wall Street was Delmonico's, a restaurant as ritzy as New York could get. In charge of the kitchen was a Frenchman called Charles Ranhofer, but he was no run-of-the-mill French chef: he'd been sent to Paris aged 12 to study pastry and by 16 he was running a kitchen for Charles d'Hénin, the Count of Alsace, at his ancestral home of Château de Bourlémont in Lorraine. By 20 he was cooking in New York for the Russian consul and in 1862, still only 26, he was in charge of Delmonico's.

Ranhofer liked to invent and New York was the perfect playground. He was able to combine classic French techniques with New World pizzazz to draw a heady crowd, including the likes of Theodore Roosevelt, Mark Twain and Oscar Wilde. Ranhofer liked to name new dishes after his favourite diners and had already been responsible for Lobster Duke Alexis (a rich bisque made for the Russian Emperor), Veal Pie à la Dickens (yes, that Dickens) and a pistachio-crusted chicken dish named after French President Sadi Carnot. He's credited with making Baked Alaska the dish it is today (see page 198) and we'll hear about another of his innovations when we come to Lobster Thermidor on page 138. The man was the Heston Blumenthal of his day, the perfect combination of showmanship and technique. He also loved a challenge.

One particular day around 1890 the challenge was set him by a Delmonico's regular, a stockbroker called LeGrand Lockwood Benedict. Having done a few deals in the morning, LeGrand settled down to lunch with his wife Sarah. It is now that the story gets hazy. Some say it was LeGrand himself who asked Ranhofer to show him something new, others that it was Sarah who, with the maître d', discussed a concoction of poached eggs, hollandaise, ham and bread. This latter version was described in a letter to *The New York Times* magazine in 1967 by a Mabel C Butler, who claimed to be related to Sarah Benedict. Mabel was contradicting an article by the paper's food expert Craig Claiborne, which reported that the dish was first made by a Commodore E C Benedict while living in France. To this day descendants of both Benedict families claim the legacy.

In yet another variant, the inspiration is a New York stockbroker called Lemuel Benedict, alleged to have been served the eggs in the Waldorf Hotel some years later (1894) when he walked in demanding a hangover cure.

Whatever the truth may be, in 1894 Ranhofer published his great work, *The Epicurean*, and included a recipe for Eggs à la Benedick [sic]. In so doing he effectively claimed the dish as his own creation. Two years later it appeared in Fannie Farmer's revised edition of the bestselling *Boston Cooking-School Cook Book*. While inclusion in Ranhofer's book put the dish firmly on the road to international culinary fame, Farmer's endorsement meant that it reached nearly every housewife in the country. At some point it even attained the status of having its own special day – in the United States 16 April is National Eggs Benedict Day.

The dish's popularity – at any time of the day and with or without a hangover – has led to copy after copy. Variations range from Eggs Florentine (with the addition of spinach) through Eggs Provençale (the hollandaise is replaced by béarnaise sauce) to Artichoke Benedict (the eggs nest on the leaves of a globe artichoke rather than a muffin). The Irish even have a version which includes corned beef.

 # Eggs Benedict

'Cut some muffins into halves crosswise, toast them without allowing to brown, then place a round of cooked ham an eighth of an inch thick and of the same diameter as the muffins on each half. Heat in a moderate oven and put a poached egg on each toast. Cover the whole with hollandaise sauce.'

— EGGS Á LA BENEDICK, FROM *THE EPICUREAN* BY CHARLES RANHOFER, 1894

Serves 4–6

- 3 tablespoons white wine vinegar
- 4 large free-range eggs
- 2 English muffins
- 4 slices of Serrano or Bayonne ham

For the hollandaise
- 3 tablespoons white wine vinegar
- 6 peppercorns
- 1 bay leaf
- 2 egg yolks
- 125g butter
- salt and freshly ground black pepper
- lemon juice

- To make the hollandaise sauce, put the vinegar in a small saucepan with the peppercorns and bay leaf. Reduce the vinegar over a high heat until there is only 1 tablespoon left. Strain the liquid, removing the peppercorns and the bay leaf. Put the egg yolks in a food processor with the vinegar reduction. Gently melt the butter in a saucepan over a medium heat so that the butter solids fall to the bottom of the pan. Turn the food processor on and slowly pour the butter on to the egg yolks with the motor still running. The sauce will start to thicken. When only the butter solids are left, stop. If the sauce is too thick, add a little hot water. Season to taste with salt and pepper and a little lemon juice.

- Bring a deep saucepan containing at least 2 litres water to the boil and add the vinegar. Break the eggs into four separate cups or ramekins. Slice the muffins and toast. Briskly swirl the water until it forms a vortex and carefully add an egg. It will curl round and set to a neat circle. Cook for 2–3 minutes, then remove with a slotted spoon. Repeat with the other eggs, one at a time, re-whisking the water as you add the eggs. Spread some hollandaise sauce over each muffin, place a slice of ham on top and finish with a poached egg. Spoon over the remaining hollandaise and serve.

Reuben
Sandwich

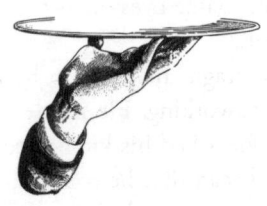

New York City has given the world many great things: skyscrapers, yellow taxis, the best movie set on the planet. And, in the combination of a fist of pastrami, tangy piquant dressing and melted cheese all held in place by two thin slices of firm rye bread, it has introduced us to the King Kong of sandwiches.

Before we get to the Reuben's classic New York beginnings, let's put the sandwich in perspective. People had been using bread to bulk out a meal ever since it was invented. Back in the Middle Ages it was used as the base to eat from, with slabs of bread known as 'trenchers' serving as plates as well as being part of the meal. However, the word 'sandwich' was first recorded in 1762 by the historian Edward Gibbon, in an obvious tribute to John Montagu, the 4th Earl of Sandwich.

Montagu held positions of power as far reaching as Postmaster General and First Lord of the Admiralty. His service record, however, was shaky and he was eventually sacked from the navy for incompetence: some even hold him responsible for Britain's defeat in the American War of Independence in 1776. But long after these battles were fought and lost, his name lives on as the originator of our most beloved lunch.

Ineffectual Montagu may have been, but he was dedicated and hardworking. He needed food that didn't interrupt him, so he asked his kitchen to slap some meat between slices of bread that he could munch away at his desk. Now, things consumed alone at work don't often gain notoriety, and many believe that Montagu took his love of the sandwich with him on his other pursuits. One of these was cards. Montagu is rumoured to have been a passionate gambler and, rather than leave the table to eat, he used to call for his bread and meat combination during games. Other players began to copy him, asking for 'the same as Sandwich' and eventually just 'a Sandwich'. The name stuck, Gibbon reported it and there it is. Some things just make perfect sense.

Now fast-forward 150 years to 1914. Montagu's poor performance at the Admiralty has allowed the United States of America to evolve and New York to thrive. Arnold Reuben's delicatessen has opened its doors and into it one night comes an actress who's working with Charlie Chaplin on a movie. 'Reuben, make me a sandwich, make it a combination, I'm so hungry I could eat a brick,' she says. He slices a loaf of rye on the bias and produces an enormous sandwich with turkey, ham, coleslaw, melted cheese and a tangy Russian dressing. She eats it, she loves it, she brings her friends back to try it and it promptly becomes Reuben's special.

This actress's name is variously recorded as Annette Seelos or Anna Selos and sadly we know nothing else about her. There is also no record of her in any Chaplin movie – but as he was involved in around 40 movies in 1914 alone, that perhaps isn't too surprising.

Another version of this story leaves the bread out of the original creation and credits Arnold Reuben Jr with turning his father's special into a sandwich. This was in 1935, when New York's workforce was returning to offices after the Great Depression and had less time to sit and mull over their future. The sandwich could be eaten fast or wrapped to go – the choice was yours. At first Reuben Jr made his sandwich with ham, but later corned beef was an option; opinion is still divided over which is best. Myself, I like pastrami.

Food folklore also tells a tale about Reuben Kulakofsky, a Lithuanian-born grocer from Omaha, Nebraska. He allegedly created a sandwich for a group of friends for their late-night poker games in around 1925, using – among other ingredients – corned beef and sauerkraut. The sandwich's fame spread when one of the group, Charles Schimmel, put it on the bar menu at his hotel, the Blackstone.

New Yorkers rubbish any Nebraskan claims to the sandwich they love so much, but it was after a Nebraskan won a national sandwich competition in 1956 with his version of the Reuben that it became part of the food language of America. The Nebraskan recipe produced quite a thin sandwich, however, and it may be that New Yorkers can take credit for turning it into the 'skyscraper' we know today. Whatever the truth may be, the Reuben is quintessentially New York: big, bold and colourful with a melting pot of flavours – Russian dressing, Germanic rye and, just to round it off, Swiss cheese. Today we are seeing the growth of New York-style delis across Britain and France, but if there's not a Reuben Sandwich on the menu, don't bother.

 # Reuben Sandwich

This is a great weekend brunch sandwich as it is mighty filling and you will need some way to toast the sandwich together slightly if you can. You can just toast the bread separately and layer it up but the cheese does need melting.

Serves 4

- 2 tablespoons butter
- 8 slices of firm rye bread
- 8 slices of Ogleshield cheese (made by the Montgomery dairy)
- 12 ultra thin slices of pastrami
- 100g coleslaw

For the dressing
- 150ml good-quality mayonnaise
- 50ml chilli sauce
- 2 tablespoons soured cream
- 2 tablespoons freshly chopped parsley
- 1 tablespoon very finely chopped mild Spanish onion
- 1 tablespoon finely chopped gherkin
- a dash of lemon juice
- ½ teaspoon horseradish sauce
- a dash of Worcestershire sauce

- Combine all the dressing ingredients in a bowl and mix well.

- Preheat a griddle pan over a medium heat or if you have panini toaster then set it to medium.

- Butter your rye bread lightly on just one side. Turn the bread over and spread the Russian dressing on the other side. Put one slice of cheese on the dressed side of bread. Then put three slices of pastrami on top. Next add a good spoonful of coleslaw, then one more slice of cheese on top. Place a piece of rye bread on top with the buttered side facing out.

- Grill the sandwiches in the griddle pan until both sides are golden brown and the cheese is melted – about 8 minutes per side. If you have a panini toaster then close it up and toast for 4–5 minutes. Serve hot with a pile of napkins.

Beef Carpaccio

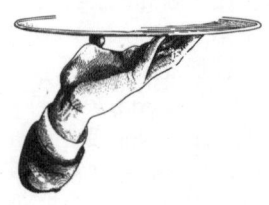

There is something very macho and impressive about ordering Beef Carpaccio and something caveman-like about eating it. It seems to recall some primitive aspect of our hunter-gatherer spirit. However, it does present certain aesthetic problems. It just won't do to throw a slab of bleeding cow flesh down on to a plate and charge top dollar for the pleasure. It takes a great chef to transform something as brutal as raw meat into a dish that is sublime and sophisticated. Beef Carpaccio is such a dish and yet its creator Giuseppe Cipriani wasn't a chef, but a barman – and what a barman!

Cipriani opened Harry's Bar in Venice in 1931. Before that he had worked as a bartender at the Hotel Europa, where a young American by the name of Harry Pickering was a regular. One day Pickering stopped coming in and when Cipriani caught up with him to ask why, he was told that the young man's family had discovered his drinking habits and cut him off financially. Cipriani immediately lent him 10,000 lire. Two years went by before Pickering returned to the Europa bar. He ordered a drink, gave Cipriani 50,000 lire and told him to use it to open a bar bearing his name. So, legend has it, Harry's Bar was born.

Harry's Bar soon became the talk of the town and Cipriani found himself serving cocktails to the rich and famous of Venice and the world, including Alfred Hitchcock, Orson Welles, Charlie Chaplin and Noël Coward. The bar also offered a small menu of food classics: pasta, some simple seafood and a few meat dishes. So when one day in 1950 Cipriani was making his famous dry martini for one of his regulars it was no surprise that the talk should turn to food.

Although she was wealthy and aristocratic, Countess Amalia Nani Mocenigo was not a well woman; she suffered from fatigue and regular bouts of illness. Her doctor had suggested that she ought to eat more red meat. (Some versions of the story say that the doctor was a vegetarian and recommended raw meat.) Either way, the Countess told Cipriani, she didn't care for red meat; she found it tough and hard to digest.

Cipriani's brilliance lay in his being a great innovator. As he poured the Countess's martini, his mind went into overdrive. He went to the kitchen, took a piece of his finest steak and cut it into the thinnest slices he could. He then pounded it even thinner, bashing each slice out to less than a millimetre thick. When laid on a plate the slices still looked rather unappetizing, so he quickly threw together a piquant mustard sauce to cover it.

How the Countess felt about the dish has never been recorded. But the cocktail-loving crowd of Harry's Bar adored it. It was sleek, light and effortless to eat. Like a dozen oysters on the table, it forced people to conquer some kind of primal fear: the fear of consuming raw flesh, like our earliest ancestors. This was about as rock 'n' roll as food got.

Cipriani named the dish after the Venetian painter Vittore Carpaccio. Although less well known to the wider world than his contemporary Bellini, he was highly regarded in Venice and there had been an exhibition of his works that very year. His use of vivid reds against an otherwise pale, creamy background had caught Cipriani's artist's eye – he saw something of the sixteenth-century palette in the way the mustard sauce and the deep red beef intermingled on the plate.

As with all great and simple things Beef Carpaccio was widely copied. Thanks to Harry's Bar's international clientele and the constant flood of tourists to one of the world's most spectacular cities, the dish took flight across Italy and to England, France and America. All it required was the right setting and the right reason to eat it, so soon every bar, cafe and restaurant was offering it to those with pockets deep enough to pay for it.

A footnote to the story of Harry's Bar: another famous regular in the 1940s and '50s was Ernest Hemingway. He mentioned the bar many times in his novel *Across the River and into the Trees*. Cipriani later wrote that people often remarked on the amount of promotion Hemingway gave Harry's. Oh no, he always replied, 'It was me and my bar that promoted him. They gave him the Nobel prize afterwards, not before.'

These days the term 'Carpaccio' may be used to describe a dish consisting of thinly sliced strips of any ingredient, but it would be foolhardy to try it yourself with any meat other than with beef or perhaps venison of whose provenance you can be absolutely sure. If you can do that – and you have a very sharp carving knife capable of producing wafer-thin slices – a Carpaccio is the perfect excuse to celebrate the newly invigorated passion for Great British beef.

Beef Carpaccio

It goes without saying that only the very best beef will do for this recipe and I advise getting to know your butcher a little before you purchase it too. It's always nice to be able to look a person in the eye when you buy something from them that you intend to eat uncooked! In terms of presentation get creative and evoke the spirit of the Renaissance that Carpaccio was very much a part of.

Serves 4

- 3 big sprigs of rosemary
- 500g whole fillet beef
- Maldon sea salt
- freshly ground black pepper
- 100g baby spinach
- Parmesan cheese (optional)

For the dressing
- 2 egg yolks
- 4 tablespoons olive oil
- 1 tablespoon Dijon mustard
- salt and freshly ground black pepper

- Finely chop the rosemary and sprinkle over the beef fillet with a handful of Maldon sea salt and some freshly ground black pepper. Roll the meat on a board so it's fully coated and then sear in a hot pan for 10 seconds on either side.

- Wrap the beef in clingfilm and put it in the freezer for 30 minutes – this will make it easier to cut.

- Remove the beef from the freezer and cut it into thin slices, stretching out each slice with the smooth side of the knife.

- Mix the dressing ingredients together in a bowl until they thicken and season with salt and pepper to taste.

- Place a handful of spinach leaves on each plate, top with about four slices of beef and pour over the dressing. You can add a couple of shavings of Parmesan cheese if you wish.

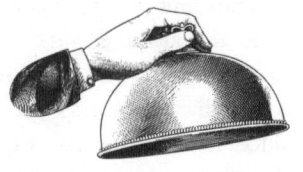

Tournedos Rossini

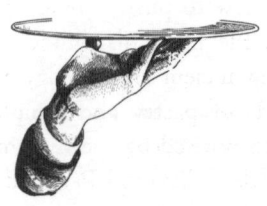

Every industry has its unique pioneers, individuals who single-handedly move the level of ability and knowledge forward so significantly that nothing is ever quite the same again. In the culinary world Marie-Antoine Carême stands out as the man responsible for turning cooking into the art it is today. He has become known as the 'king of chefs and the chef of kings', a moniker given to him by the world's press over the two hundred years since he set the culinary world alight. Today much of his influence is seen in the little things – a sauce, a certain cut of meat or maybe just a garnish – but don't be fooled: his influence is huge. One of his greatest creations, with its combination of fillet steak, foie gras and truffles, is as decadent as it is delicious. Just one taste of the accompanying Madeira sauce and you are transported, like a time traveller, back to the heady days of France under Napoleon Bonaparte.

Apprenticed at 14 to a successful pâtissier by the name of Sylvain Bailly, Carême showed such talent that by the beginning of the nineteenth century, aged just 19, he had left to set up shop on his own.

Carême knew how to push people's buttons, to excite them with food. He filled his window with towers of sweet magic, using ancient archaeology as his inspiration to build pyramids of pastry and temples of marzipan. His skill was soon noticed by the diplomat and gourmet Charles Maurice de Talleyrand-Périgord (Talleyrand for short), who hired him to create impressive desserts for a meeting of the powermongers of a new Europe. Carême used the opportunity to extend his knowledge to all areas of cooking and the future 'chef of kings' was soon the chef of an emperor – Napoleon.

As the little Emperor's influence extended across Europe, the name of his chef grew with it. So much so that following the fall of Napoleon in 1815 Carême was able to work first for the Prince Regent in England, then for Tsar Alexander I and finally come back to Paris in the employ of James Mayer de Rothschild, a wealthy banker at the centre of the new French elite.

Meanwhile, on the other side of the Alps, another genius was growing up. Gioachino Antonio Rossini had the same pioneering spirit as Carême and the same passion for his music that Carême had for his cooking. He began composing in 1810, and in 1816, when he was still only 24, his masterwork *The Barber of Seville* redefined what Italian opera was all about.

The composer was soon travelling the world with invitations from far and wide. His now famous appetite and knowledge of cooking eventually guided him to the House of Rothschild, where he became great friends with the banker's master chef. On every visit to the Rothschilds Rossini would make a beeline to the kitchen to talk and cook with his kindred spirit. The mists of time have hidden the answer to which of them came up with the dish that would eventually bear the composer's name, but the clever money is on Rossini, with Carême's flair helping it to evolve and become a thing of beauty.

The word 'tournedos' is now used to describe a cut of meat from the lower back and some believe it derives from *tourner le dos*, meaning 'to turn one's back': Rossini is reputed to have shouted this at an unworthy chef at Le Café Anglais who attempted to recreate the dish for him one day. What is more certain is that Carême cooked Tournedos Rossini many times with his friend and he is generally credited with naming it after the great composer.

The dish quickly arrived on the menus of the big Paris hotels and restaurants and then, as the world got smaller and people moved around its surface with ease, they took it east and west. For three decades from the 1950s it was a grandstand restaurant and dinner-party dish that never failed to impress. Then, in the 1980s, the old ways drifted out of favour, to be replaced by faster, lighter cooking from around the world. But now, with our renewed love affair with the past, it is back.

Great works of art will always outlive their creator and just as *The Barber of Seville* will be sung as long as Italy has operas (not my words, but those of a certain Ludwig van Beethoven), so people with passionate appetites for luxurious food will always order Tournedos Rossini.

Tournedos Rossini

This is a big, gutsy dish in the grand tradition of classic French cuisine. The key is the technical cooking of the steaks and the rich, velvety texture of the sauce. Serve it with a nice bottle of Burgundy and a big fat smile. You can swap mushrooms for the truffle if you are not feeling that extravagant and if you are in disagreement with the way foie gras is produced then you can leave it out altogether.

Serves 4

- 1 tablespoon olive oil
- 1 tablespoon butter
- 4 x 200g beef fillet steaks (go for the centre cut if you can)
- salt and freshly ground black pepper
- 4 x 50g slices of foie gras, no more than 1cm wide
- 4 slices of good-quality white bread, 1cm wide
- freshly chopped chervil (optional)

For the sauce
- 1 tablespoon port
- 2 tablespoons brandy
- 2 tablespoons Madeira, plus extra for braising
- 100ml veal stock or very dark beef stock
- 2 garlic cloves, very finely sliced
- 1 truffle, thinly sliced

- Add the oil and butter to a hot skillet or frying pan. Season your steaks with salt and pepper on both sides. When the butter is foaming add the steaks and cook over a high heat for 2–3 minutes on each side until the meat is nicely sealed. Remove from the pan and keep warm.

- Add the slices of foie gras to the hot pan, sear them very quickly then remove them from the pan and put on kitchen paper.

- Deglaze the pan with the port, brandy and Madeira. Once you have got all that lovely flavour out, add the stock and reduce the heat. Let the sauce bubble away until it starts to thicken.

- In a separate pan add a dash of Madeira and the garlic, then add the sliced truffle. Braise gently for a couple of minutes then add the reduced sauce to the pan.

- Toast the bread. Place each steak on the toast, top with the foie gras and pour over the truffle sauce. I like to finish the dish with a little chopped chervil but you can leave it out if you wish and just tuck in.

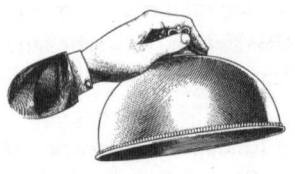

Beef Stroganoff

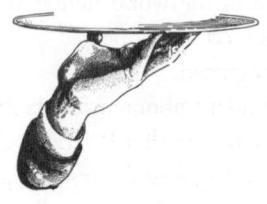

Few dishes can be more satisfying than tender strips of beef fillet and mushrooms coated in smoky, piquant cream, all embraced by soft, sweet onions. It's no wonder that the rich and powerful of nineteenth-century Russia were crazy about it: it reeks of money and power. The fact that, in its classic form, it requires the most expensive cut of meat is a clear indication of its heritage.

In the 1890s the Russian Empire was strong. In the west it covered most of Eastern Europe; to the east its influence spread down into northern China; and it had a modest 127 million people under its control. As in all empires there was great economic disparity – while many starved there were a significant few who lived in luxury. One such man was Count Pavel Stroganoff, a diplomat and gourmet who often entertained his friends with extravagant feasts. His chef, Charles Brière, achieved a certain notoriety and a light-hearted competition was organized among the great families of St Petersburg to see whose chef could produce the finest dish. Brière's entry, Beef Stroganoff, was crowned winner and news of its success was published in the prestigious *L'Art Culinaire*. Believe it or not, in 1891 this was the only magazine in the world aimed at the professional chef and once something appeared in its pages it was internationally recognized.

We can be confident about most of this story, but we can't be 100 per cent sure that Brière invented the dish. It was reproduced in *Larousse Gastronomique* in the 1930s under his name, and has remained there ever since. However, some believe that it is much older and may have been made for a previous Count Stroganoff by the name of Grigory. Grigory was elderly and losing his teeth, so he could chew only the softest and tenderest beef: it may be that his unnamed and uncredited chef created this simple dish to satisfy his needs.

Grigory died in 1857, so it could be his version of the dish that found its way into the 1861 edition of *A Gift to Young Housewives* by Elena Molokhovets. Containing not just recipes but general cooking advice and kitchen etiquette as well, this book was the essential kitchen purchase for any aspiring Russian housewife and it was reissued every year from 1861 until 1917. Molokhovets' Stroganoff was more rustic than the one we know today – it had no tomato or shallots and was essentially a spiced-up soured-cream sauce with chunks rather than strips of beef – but the similarities are clear and it almost certainly inspired Briere to produce his version. Incidentally, the first record of the dish containing tomato appeared in 1912, alongside the first mention of serving it with straw fries.

Thanks to its inclusion in these influential publications, Beef Stroganoff's fame spread and it became part of the everyday repertoire of many chefs. The Russian predilection for naming things after their noble patrons meant Charles Briere himself began to fade into history, but the popularity of the dish never wavered.

It made its debut in American literature in John MacPherson's *Mystery Chef's Own Cook Book* in 1934. Five years later it was cited in Diana Ashley's *Where to Dine in '39* as being popular in two long-since-vanished Russian eateries in New York. But it took the two world wars of the twentieth century to bring it global recognition. Servicemen stationed in China and Russia came across Beef Stroganoff and loved it. On their return home they sought out the ingredients and as a result it became popular in America, Britain and France almost simultaneously. American chefs left their own mark by adapting it to include the country's favourite side dish, French fries. Then, during the 1950s and '60s, Beef Stroganoff became a favourite dinner-party choice of sophisticated Americans – like Veal Orloff (see page 78), it owes much of its fame to the efforts of Julia Child.

Stroganoff was originally served on its own without side vegetables but, thanks to Chinese influence, is now generally accompanied by rice or noodles. As it moved from country to country it was easily adapted. Versions exist for all sorts of Stroganoffs, such as a Brazilian-inspired one with ketchup instead of tomato paste, a Swedish one with a large beef sausage instead of fillet and a Japanese one with a little touch of soy. In the end it doesn't matter as long as the essence is the same. It is the tender beef and earthy mushrooms with that creamy punchy sauce, flavoured with paprika or mustard or both, that hold this dish up high among the gastronomical elite, turning a soldiers' favourite into a culinary classic.

Beef Stroganoff

This version is the full ticket – it's a gift to you from Lawrence Keogh, former head chef at the iconic London restaurant, The Wolseley. It's packed to the brim with power and punch. It's a dish that takes minutes to make so ensure you have everything ready to go and then just throw the pan in the sink and tuck in. I like to buy a whole beef fillet and trim the tail off, freeze it and use the rest for a Beef Wellington, this way you are always prepared for Stroganoff time.

Serves 4

- 450g beef fillet strips, cut from the tail end
- salt and freshly ground black pepper
- 1 teaspoon hot paprika
- 2 teaspoons sweet paprika, plus extra for serving
- vegetable oil, for frying
- 30g butter
- 2 shallots, finely chopped
- 115g button mushrooms, thinly sliced
- 1 teaspoon tomato purée
- 50ml white wine vinegar
- 75ml white wine
- 200ml double cream
- 115g dill pickle, cut into thin strips
- 125ml soured cream
- 1 tablespoon finely chopped flatleaf parsley
- 165g basmati rice, cooked according to the packet instructions

- Sprinkle the beef with salt and pepper and roll it in the two paprikas.

- Heat a frying pan and add a little vegetable oil. Flash-fry the strips of beef until they are rare – about 2–3 minutes, then remove them from the pan and put in a sieve allowing any juices to drip into a bowl. Set aside.

- Add the butter and shallots to the pan that you cooked the beef in. Then add the mushrooms and cook for a further minute. Add the tomato purée and cook for a couple of minutes. Stir well, then add the white wine vinegar and reduce the mixture until all the liquid has evaporated.

- Add the white wine and reduce the liquid by half. Pour in the cream and bring to the boil. Season with salt and pepper. Add the beef and the cooking juices and warm through but do not boil – the beef needs no more cooking.

- Serve with the dill pickle on top, a drizzle of soured cream, a dusting of paprika, a scattering of flatleaf parsley and the rice on the side.

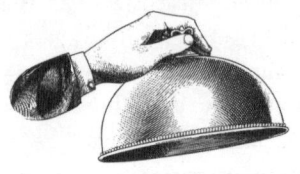

Beef Wellington

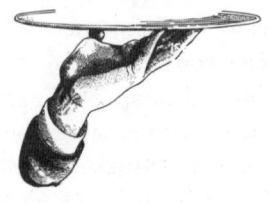

Nothing symbolizes a special occasion like a perfect pink piece of beef fillet covered in mushrooms and ham, then wrapped in a pancake and puff pastry. The Beef Wellington is one of the most stunning pieces of British cuisine in existence; it is also one of the most complicated to get right. It requires military timing, precision and planning, so in the wrong hands it can easily become a culinary Waterloo. Thus it is fitting that its beginnings are intrinsically linked to one the greatest military strategists in history.

Sadly, British culinary pride is a recent phenomenon and there is no written record of Beef Wellington's development. Its name is assumed to refer to the man who crushed Napoleon at the Battle of Waterloo, but some food historians claim it is more to do with the dish's resemblance to a Wellington boot. We are certain that the Duke of Wellington liked his beef – documents make reference to his army consuming 300 bullocks a day during the battle-weary month of November 1813 – but no clear story of the first Beef Wellington has ever been told.

In culinary terms, Arthur Wellesley, 1st Duke of Wellington, could not have been more different from his great adversary. As we shall see under Chicken Marengo (see page 96), Napoleon was a foodie who organized huge feasts to celebrate victories. Wellington, on the other hand, was a pragmatist with little passion for food. After his famous victory in June 1815, he had plans for fortifications and peaceful restructuring in mind; it is unlikely that any kind of celebratory meal took place.

Nevertheless, Wellington returned to England triumphant and was given medals and titles, even becoming Prime Minister in 1828. So it is no huge surprise that an enterprising chef should have chosen to create a magnificent dish in his honour. Britain's history of cooking pieces of meat wrapped in pastry dates back as far as the fifteenth century, when records show early Tudor recipes using basic flour-and-water dough to create cooking vessels in which to stew venison and beef. The great kitchens of Henry VIII are a testament to pie-making of this kind; many a banquet was treated to the tearing off of a pastry lid, with the circle of inedible crust being used as a serving plate for the stewed meat. Beef was not an everyday ingredient – the vast majority of the population would have been eating pork if they could get their hands on any meat at all. In the grander kitchens, though, culinary ways were developing and, despite the historical conflicts between the two nations, French techniques were becoming more widely used. So by the 1830s wrapping the finest piece of beef in the most technically demanding of all pastries must have seemed a logical way to impress.

Beef Wellington remained largely a British recipe for quite some time. There is an obvious reason for its lack of take-up in France, although they do a remarkably similar *filet de boeuf en croûte* and it's possible that the French recipe came first, inspiring an unknown British chef to adapt it. The French version is more likely to use foie gras instead of a mushroom duxelle to coat the beef.

In America it needed an unlikely hero to help it break into the recipe repertoire. In 1970 President Richard Nixon, later forced to stand down due to his involvement in the Watergate scandal, declared Beef Wellington his favourite dish, having come across it on state visits to the United Kingdom and been won over by the delights of its iron-rich, pastry-covered charm.

Its return to the British home-cooking scene came around the same time. Home entertaining was now hugely popular, with the general increase in the standard of living making it easier to cook for fun rather than necessity. Cookery books and TV chefs proliferated. The construction of a Beef Wellington made for good small-screen entertainment and filled the viewer with enthusiastic confidence at being able to replicate it at their next dinner party. Chefs and cookery writers were soon producing short-cut versions and it became acceptable to leave out the mushrooms, or to use shortcrust instead of puff pastry. It was also possible to buy pastry ready-made in supermarkets, which made the dish a great deal more accessible. Before long anything meaty wrapped in pastry became a 'Wellington', with recipes featuring everything from chicken to wild duck.

A dish like Beef Wellington really deserves a 'eureka' creation moment, but some things were simply meant to be and the romantic in me likes to believe that this recipe discovered us rather than the other way around. Its name has done nothing for Anglo-French culinary relations, but try not to worry – just be glad it found us!

Beef Wellington

This recipe is based on the classic preparation with a few time-savers and the absence of foie gras to make it a little easier to cook in Britain. If you can get some just spread it over the beef before you add the layer of mushroom pâté.

Serves 6

For the pancakes
- 3 free-range eggs
- 6 tablespoons plain flour
- 150ml milk
- knob of butter

For the beef wellington
- 500g beef fillet, middle section
- freshly ground black pepper
- 375g packet ready-rolled puff pastry
- 4 slices of prosciutto
- 75g smooth mushroom pâté
- 1 free-range egg, plus 1 free-range egg yolk

- To make the pancakes, put the eggs and flour in a bowl and whisk together. Gradually add the milk, whisking constantly, to create a smooth batter. Put a frying pan on the hob over a high heat. Add the butter and, once melted, a ladleful of the batter, tilting the pan to thinly coat the base. When the underside of the pancake is cooked and golden, turn it over and cook the other side. Tip the pancake out on to a plate covered with baking parchment. Repeat this process to make another pancake and layer with parchment.

- Season the beef fillet with black pepper then put in a frying pan over a high heat. Turn the fillet to ensure even cooking. Remove when browned on each side and leave to rest in a warm place.

- Roll out the puff pastry to 5mm thick. Place the pancakes in the centre of the pastry. Arrange the prosciutto evenly over the pancakes. Spread the pâté over one side of the beef and then place the meat pâté-side down on to the prosciutto. Beat the egg and egg yolk together in a bowl, then brush the egg over the clear area of the pancakes and pastry and fold round to enclose the beef. Put the Wellington seam-side down on to a baking tray and brush with the beaten egg. Put in the fridge to cool for 30 minutes.

- Preheat the oven to 200°C/Gas Mark 6.

- Remove the Wellington from the fridge and brush with egg once more. Bake in the oven for 25 minutes, or until the pastry is golden, then remove and leave to rest on a serving plate for 10 minutes (longer if you do not like your beef rare).

- Serve slices of the Beef Wellington with gravy and cooked seasonal vegetables on the side.

Steak Diane

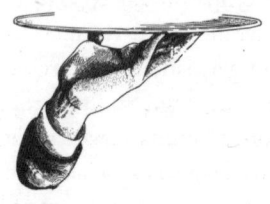

Steak Diane presents something of a conundrum. It is a luxurious dish dripping in masculine meaty flavours, covered in a rich, buttery sauce with just a dash of brandy, then flambéed. However, it is named after not only a goddess but the most austere goddess of the entire entourage of Greek gods.

Diana was a maiden who vowed never to marry; instead she gave her passion to hunting and to the worship of the moon. She is always portrayed as slim and beautiful, often accompanied by a deer or some hunting dogs – never, it would seem, draped in cream and alcohol with occasional slices of truffle. But her association with hunting led to her name being given to a strongly flavoured, peppery sauce which went well with tougher game meats such as venison.

The earliest written record of a Diane Sauce comes in *Le Guide Culinaire*, the masterwork of French chef Auguste Escoffier, published in 1903 and translated into English in 1907. Escoffier had ignited the London culinary scene with his classical French cooking and his writing had united the gastronomic world by recording over a thousand recipes for other chefs to read and copy. He suggests only venison as an accompaniment to Sauce Diane, which he describes as a 'poivrade sauce, thinned by means of a little beaten cream, and garnished with crescents of truffle and hard-boiled white of egg'. So he probably evolved the recipe himself from a familiar and widely used peppercorn sauce. The culinary leap to associating the sauce with beef and in particular with very fine slivers of beef came quite a few decades later – in New York in the 1950s.

Exactly which kitchen and which chef first struck upon the idea of taking a sauce intended for venison and pouring it over a thin piece of pounded steak no one really knows.

At least four establishments are possible candidates: the Drake Hotel, the 21 Club, the Sherry-Netherland Hotel and the Colony Restaurant. Jane Nickerson, food editor of *The New York Times*, reported in an article published in 1953 that 'Nino of the Drake' claimed to have introduced the recipe to New York and to the entire United States; but other sources, including Jean Anderson's *The American Century Cookbook*, published in 1997, associate it with 21 and the Colony. A former speakeasy, the 21 Club was the late-night haunt of stars such as Frank Sinatra and Humphrey Bogart, who came after an appearance on a Broadway stage and stayed until they were removed; in the Colony you were more likely to find Vanderbilts, Astors and Windsors. It was often said that your status in New York depended purely on where you sat at the Colony. There were banquettes for the rich and famous and an area called 'the doghouse' for the socially less desirable. The owner Gene Cavallero knew the power of publicity and allowed society journalists to eat for free; the fact that he had his own public relations man was a sign of what restaurants would become in the future.

At that time, a lot of food was served from dining carts, but the most exciting restaurants – including 21 and the Colony – were fronted by a maître d' who cooked a few select dishes out in the dining room by your table. These were often the eye-catching menu items that required a touch of flame – think Crêpes Suzette or Bananas Foster – and Steak Diane was no different. Diners could watch the meat being beaten wafer thin, then flash-fried in plenty of pepper and set to rest while the mushrooms were cooked in the same pan and flambéed in brandy before the sauce was finished with cream and mustard. Simple but sensational, Steak Diane's fame quickly spread not only around New York but across the whole of America and into Europe, as other restaurateurs recognized a good thing and put it on their own menus.

For almost a decade Steak Diane enjoyed full iconic status. Then economics stepped in and changed the course of the dish's life story. During the 1960s and '70s rents in New York began to rise, floor space in restaurants was suddenly at a premium and soon diners were sitting elbow to elbow to maximize turnover. The opportunity to see bright purple flames leaping up and dancing round the dining room vanished. Soon afterwards, fire-safety legislation and sprinkler systems put a stop to dining-room flames for good.

Steak Diane fell into decline as a restaurant dish and only larger establishments were able to devote the space and staff to serving it tableside. At home it is a recipe best saved for a special occasion. It is by no means the most elegant-looking plate of food, but boy does the flavour pack a god-like punch.

 # Steak Diane

This is a properly old school dish. It conjures up a time when celebrities would dine out and be snapped enjoying fancy Russian cigarettes with their glamorous co-stars. It is important to burn off the brandy not just for the excitement levels but that final burst of heat just adds a toasty note to the sauce, which is important.

Serves 4

- 4 x 175g sirloin steaks
- salt and freshly ground black pepper
- 50g unsalted butter
- 2 shallots, finely chopped
- 110g button mushrooms
- 50ml brandy
- 250ml double cream
- 1 teaspoon Dijon mustard
- 2 teaspoons Worcestershire sauce
- 2 tablespoons freshly chopped flatleaf parsley
- vegetable oil, for deep frying
- 3 large baking potatoes, peeled and finely sliced into matchsticks

- Flatten the steaks with a meat hammer or a rolling pin until 1.5–2cm thick. Season well with salt and pepper.

- Cook half the butter in a frying pan over a medium heat until it foams. Add the steaks and fry for 2 minutes on each side for medium-rare or as long as you wish to get the steaks as you like them. Remove from the pan and set aside to keep warm.

- In the same pan add the remaining butter. When the butter foams add the shallots and fry until soft – about 3 minutes. Don't let them get crispy. Add the mushrooms and cook for a further 2 minutes or so until they have started to give up their water and soften. Pour in the brandy, carefully light with a match and let the flames subside. Add the cream, mustard and Worcestershire sauce and reduce for a couple of minutes or until you have the consistency of single cream. Stir in the parsley and check the seasoning.

- Add the steaks to warm through but do not let the mixture boil.

- To make the fries, heat the oil in a deep saucepan. When you drop a breadcrumb in and it goes brown in about 20 seconds you are ready to cook the fries. (The oil needs to be about 190°C if you have a fryer.) Lower in the potatoes and fry until brown and crispy – about 3–4 minutes. Drain on kitchen paper and season. Cook the potatoes in batches if necessary.

- Serve by placing a steak on each plate, pouring over the sauce and piling the fries on the side. You could also serve this with some buttered peas if you wish.

Veal Prince Orloff

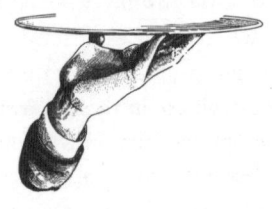

Most of us instinctively understand the difference between home cooking and fine dining. But unless we've been in the presence of presidents or kings we may not fully appreciate the giant leap to the next level of eating – grand cuisine. It's a whole new giddy atmosphere up there, where the gastronomic air is thin and the ambition of the dishes is achievable by only the very best. Veal Orloff, sometimes known as Veal Prince Orloff, belongs to this world.

It consists of a whole loin of veal roasted on the bone, then the cannon of meat removed and sliced. Between every two slices is a layer of mushrooms and a soubise of puréed onions. The meat is placed back into its bony cradle, covered in a rich béchamel sauce and plenty of cheese, then returned to the oven to brown. It is finished with ample slices of fresh truffle. As you might expect, its creator was a grand master of his art, although history has not celebrated him nearly as much as some of his peers. He was born in Provence in 1818 and his name was Urbain Dubois.

As a 14-year-old apprentice, Dubois stumbled upon one of the greatest kitchens in culinary history, that of Lord Rothschild, where Marie-Antoine Carême was in the process of changing global gastronomy forever; his adventures appear elsewhere in this book. For Dubois this presented a unique opportunity. Having learnt to prepare the grand gestures essential to a great feast, he was able to become chef to the Russian Ambassador to France, Prince Alexey Fyodorovich Orloff.

Working for Orloff provided the perfect environment for Dubois to develop his skills. He also began to examine the way food was served. At the time French banquets were served all at once, with food displayed in front of the diners like a parade of fine treasures. The problem was always keeping the hot food hot and the cold food cold; only the most organized of chefs could pull this off. The Russian style was to serve food course by course, with individual plates sent to individual diners. This may sound obvious to us today, but in the mid-nineteenth century it was revolutionary. Dubois quickly realized that this new way of working allowed for more intricate displays: the way in which plates were prepared became a matter of artistry and design as much as of culinary skill.

Veal, being expensive but delicately flavoured, was the meat of choice for the ruling classes. So it was inevitable that Dubois should create a spectacular veal dish for one of his employer's banquets. Who got to eat the first slice has not been recorded, but we do know that in a cruel twist of fate the Ambassador himself was not a huge fan. His taste ran to lighter dishes, but he could appreciate Veal Orloff's wow factor and it became a frequent feature of his entertaining menu.

In 1864 Dubois moved to the employ of another passionate gastronome, William I, King of Prussia and later the first Kaiser of a united Germany. He too wanted visual impact and Veal Orloff was just the thing. It was served many times on special occasions and the chefs of Dubois' homeland began to discover it. Dubois was a prolific writer, too; throughout his career he made methodical notes of his work and wrote eight books, the most famous of which, *La Cuisine Classique*, published in 1856, contained the recipe for Veal Orloff. Dubois' were the first cookery books to contain illustrations and diagrams of how many of his dishes were to be served. As a result he continued to influence food styling for decades after he died in 1901. He also detailed how a menu should be constructed and served, an idea later used by Auguste Escoffier in his own writings.

Veal Orloff is still occasionally served today and is often used as a illustration of old-style grand cuisine. America was first shown its power in the same way it discovered many European dishes, through the works of Julia Child. In the 1960s Child embarked on a one-woman mission to show her fellow Americans the joys of French food, and Veal Orloff was one of many thousands of recipes that featured in her umpteen television series. She came up with a version using a veal chop rather than a whole loin and also famously created a simpler (and cheaper) Turkey Orloff. These dishes soon became an indispensable feature of middle-class American dinner parties. Quite how many housewives attempted to cook an authentic Veal Orloff for their husbands is unclear, but at least they got to peer through a window to a different gastronomic world.

Veal Prince Orloff

To try Veal Orloff at home takes a brave heart and a fairly high level of culinary skill. The result is worth it, but if you don't have that much time to spend, this version uses a very nice cut of veal, the chop, which will give you a taste of Dubois' genius.

Serves 4

- 4 tablespoons butter
- 1 medium-sized onion, finely chopped
- 150g brown mushrooms, very finely sliced
- 2 tablespoons lemon juice
- salt and freshly ground black pepper
- 4 x 230g veal chops from the rack or loin (preferably from the centre and with most of the fat removed)

For the sauce
- 2 tablespoons butter
- 2 tablespoons plain flour
- 240ml milk
- 60ml double cream
- ½ teaspoon freshly grated nutmeg
- pinch of cayenne pepper
- 2 tablespoons grated Parmesan or Gruyère cheese
- 1 egg yolk

- Preheat the oven to 220°C/Gas Mark 7. Heat a large frying pan on the hob and add half the butter. When it starts foaming slightly add the onion and cook until it is soft and translucent. You don't want it to go brown. Add the mushrooms, lemon juice and salt and pepper. Keep the pan over a medium heat until the mushrooms have released most of their moisture and set aside.

- To make the cheese sauce, melt the butter in a saucepan. Add the flour slowly and keep stirring. It is important to cook out the flour or your sauce will not have the right glossy consistency – it must not brown. Remove the pan from the heat and add the milk slowly, stirring very rapidly as you do so. When the sauce is smooth return the pan to the heat and gently warm.

- Pour in the cream then add the nutmeg and cayenne and season well. Increase the heat and reduce the sauce slightly – about 5 minutes – then leave it to cool and add half of the cheese. Stir well.

- Melt the remaining butter in a large, heavy skillet. Add the veal chops and cook over medium-high heat for about 6 minutes or until nicely browned. Turn and cook for a further 6 minutes on the other side. Transfer the chops to a baking dish large enough to hold them in one layer. Spoon equal portions of the mushroom mixture over each chop. Smooth the sauce over the top with a palette knife so it covers the chops evenly.

- Lightly beat the egg yolk and add it to the cheese sauce. Spoon this over the top of the mushrooms and veal then sprinkle with the other half of the cheese. Bake the dish in the oven for about 10 minutes until the top has a nice glaze. You can even put it under the grill to brown the top up more if you wish.

- Serve each chop with plenty of sauce and some green beans.

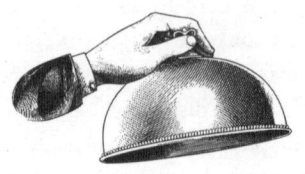

Lamb Balti

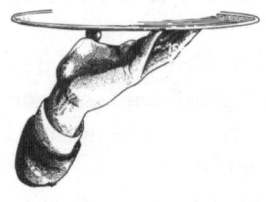

Few dishes have elevated themselves to the iconic status of the balti in such a short time. It is almost a rite of passage in some parts of Britain to 'go for a balti' and the luxurious dark gravy and melt-in-the-mouth texture of the lamb is hard to beat. The balti has five main characteristics that make it unique in Indian cuisine. The meat is always cooked off the bone and at a high temperature in the trademark metal dish. Vegetable oil is used instead of ghee and fresh spices rather than ready-made pastes and blends. Finally, it is served in the dish in which it was cooked.

The food of the Indian subcontinent is notable for its clearly defined regional nature, with drier, often game-based dishes coming from Rajasthan in the north, Kerala in the south famous for its seafood and vegetarian curries, and Goa in the southwest producing richer, gravy-based recipes. The numerous different types of curry often appear baffling, with restaurant menus requiring careful study and much explanation. So it is no surprise that some of the most famous Indian dishes, certainly in the United Kingdom, have very little to do with this complicated tradition and more to do with the desire to introduce a new country to the joys of Indian cooking. The Lamb Balti does share one thing with its Indian heritage, though. It is identified with a single area, a place with very few other gastronomic credentials, but one that since the 1970s has become synonymous with vibrant new Indian cuisine: Birmingham.

The British have had a close relationship with the subcontinent ever since the British East India Company was established in the seventeenth century. Since then the two places have traded spices, cloth, technology and people through all the various incarnations of their political associations. With this trade came, inevitably, an exchange of food. Recipes and cooking techniques travelled back and forth across the oceans to be adapted and adopted in their new homes. In Britain especially Indian recipes were modified to suit the gentler Western palate.

Even the name 'balti' is a British construction. Its connection with the dish is two-fold. First it is a small, flat-bottomed, often copper pot in which the food is cooked and served; and second it derives from a part of northern Pakistan from which some of the immigrant families of Birmingham came. Most experts discount the association with Baltistan in favour of the serving-dish theory, but it seems sensible that the two meanings should have come together to give the recipe its now familiar moniker.

The first Indian restaurant in Britain, the Hindostanee Coffee House, opened in London in 1810 and tried to give customers a taste of what would later be called the Raj: colonial decor with colonially influenced food. Unfortunately it had arrived a good century and a half too early: people weren't ready for the heavily spiced cuisine and it went bankrupt just three years later.

It wasn't until the 1960s that the United Kingdom saw a resurgence in Indian-style restaurants. The country was enjoying an economic boom and eating out was increasingly popular. An influx of immigrants from the subcontinent had given rise to small localized communities, with restaurants catering initially for their own tastes. But soon a wider public discovered this new breed of restaurant cuisine and began to delight in the thick, rich sauces and smoky breads that accompanied every meal. It should also be noted that the obvious compatibility with that other great British obsession, beer, played no small part in the restaurants' success.

The first balti is said to have been created by Mohammed Ajaib in Birmingham in 1977. His Al Faisals restaurant was certainly pioneering in the way it served its curries and very soon others were copying his style. By the mid-1980s the balti house was the predominant restaurant type in Birmingham. The area encompassing Ladypool Road, Stoney Lane and Stratford Road is still referred to as 'the Balti Triangle' and contains the highest concentration of balti restaurants in the city, as well as some of the oldest.

The fame of the balti spread throughout the United Kingdom and, to some extent, abroad. Today there are balti houses in Canada and Australia, with armies of new fans discovering the unique combination of deep, rich, slow-cooked curry with that hint of charring from the last-minute heat and the delicate sweetness from the cinnamon in the garam masala. But the balti's gastronomic heart is very much in Birmingham and some claim it is impossible to get an authentic version of the dish outside the Triangle. Purists maintain that it should be served with one large naan to be shared, but at home you can mix and match as you wish – as long as you serve it with an ice-cold beer.

 # Lamb Balti

It may have its roots in India but the balti is as British as beans on toast. This is a dish that benefits from slow, steady cooking so plan early and put the effort in. The final flourishes are what make it stand out as a balti and the deep, rich flavours from the lamb come alive with that last vibrant punch of fresh ingredients.

Serves 4

- 2 teaspoons cumin seeds
- 4 teaspoons coriander seeds
- 2 teaspoons black mustard seeds
- 2 teaspoons fennel seeds
- 2 teaspoons fenugreek seeds
- 2 dried Karachi chillies
- 2 tablespoons vegetable oil
- 1 large onion, finely chopped
- 5cm piece of fresh ginger, peeled and grated
- 5 garlic cloves, crushed
- 400g can chopped tomatoes
- 15 fresh curry leaves
- 1kg lamb shoulder or mutton, cut into large chunks
- salt
- 1 teaspoon garam masala
- a large bunch of coriander, chopped
- 3 red or green bird's eye chillies, split

- Add the spices and dried chillies to a hot, dry frying pan and toast for about 1 minute. Keep the pan moving to stop the spices burning and the mustard seeds should begin to pop. You will get a nutty heat from the pan to tell you the spices are done. Empty the spices into a spice grinder and grind to a fine powder.

- Heat the oil in a saucepan and add the onion, ginger and garlic and fry gently until the onion softens and takes on a little colour at the edges. Add the tomatoes and the curry leaves.

- Cook until the mixture thickens up slightly.

- Add the spice mixture to the pan being careful to stir it so that it doesn't stick. Add a little water if the mixture looks too dry. Add the lamb and stir. Add about a teaspoon of salt. Cook for about 5 minutes, stirring constantly to coat the lamb. Add 250ml water, put a lid on the pan and simmer for 1½ hours.

- Heat a balti pan on the hob. Transfer the lamb to it then add the garam masala, a big handful of chopped coriander and the bird's eye chillies. Cook for 3 minutes until piping hot and the chillies have just softened. If you don't have a balti pan then just add the garam masala, coriander and chillies to the original lamb pan.

- Serve with a pile of naan bread and a bucket of cold beers.

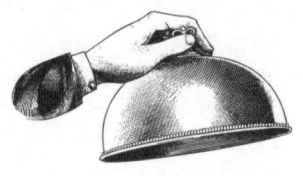

Coronation
Chicken

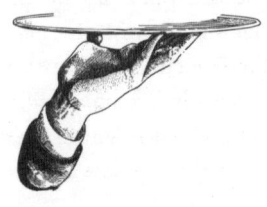

Coronation Chicken is a dish that is quintessentially British. It has a regal charm and a timeless simplicity, which have meant it's been a favourite of sandwich shops and picnics for over 50 years. It mixes the world's favourite protein with a light curry flavour that turns the humble chicken into something exotic and enticing. The yellow hue imparted by Indian spices makes it stand out from other pale, creamy bowls at the buffet table. The success it's enjoyed and the speed at which we've taken it to our hearts are down to two of Britain's greatest loves – curry and the late Queen!

On 2 June 1953 the people of Great Britain were about to crown their new queen. Preparations were meticulous and the grand procession was just that, grand. It would take the young Elizabeth from Buckingham Palace along the Mall, past roughly three million of her loyal subjects, all cheering and waving flags. It was the most spectacular outside broadcast ever to be seen on television, but the black and white cameras couldn't do justice to the thousands of pounds' worth of flowers that were carefully arranged along the route. These were the design of the country's finest florist, Constance Spry. It's not, however, for this herculean effort that she is most often connected with the Coronation, but for her culinary contribution. Constance Spry is almost invariably credited with the creation of Coronation Chicken, which is said to have been prepared for a state banquet on the big day. Some even say that the Queen herself was present.

But history has given Spry more credit than she deserves. She had made her name as a flower arranger back in the 1920s, when her use of seasonal leaves and flowers along with berries and green orchids drew huge crowds;

they loved this shift away from Victorian-style displays of asparagus ferns and carnations. Her unconventional style, making use of English countryside plants that other florists ignored, led to a new fashion in flower choice.

Spry quickly attracted some very upmarket business, allowing her to move to new premises in Mayfair, where she caught the attention of the royal family. The future Queen Elizabeth was schooled in the old ways of monarchy but she had a very modern outlook and it was her decision to ask Spry to arrange the flowers for her wedding in 1947; when Elizabeth ascended the throne five years later, Spry was the obvious choice to line the procession route with her trademark British arrangements.

In the meantime Spry had enjoyed a successful publishing career, writing several bestselling books covering both gardening and how to turn your garden into a source of delicious ingredients to cook with. For the culinary projects she had teamed up with home economist Rosemary Hume and the two had opened a cooking school together. The school flourished, as did Spry's reputation, and as a result her students were asked to prepare and host a banquet for a delegation of important foreign visitors who were in Britain for the Coronation. It was Hume who devised the menu and taught her students how to prepare the dishes. One in particular was to stand out.

A bright yellow chicken dish made with curry powder, mayonnaise and apricots, combined with just a little acidity from some lemon and vinegar, somehow captured the essence of the British Empire, with the spices reminiscent of India and the fruit introducing a taste of the Caribbean. It's worth remembering that Indian spices were unheard of in post-war Britain, so the scope for genuine multiculturalism was limited, but Hume did her best. She also deliberately and tactfully created a dish that had a touch of the exotic without being beyond the reach of a country still struggling with post-war rationing. Hume originally called the dish *Poulet reine Elizabeth*; Spry is given credit for coming up with a name that had instant popular appeal: Coronation Chicken.

The public soon found the recipe thanks to the comprehensive and helpful *Constance Spry Cookery Book*, published in 1956. Due to pressure from the publishers, J M Dent and Sons, the book was published under Spry's name alone, but I am glad to be able to do my small bit to redress the balance. The recipe's popularity spread like wildfire; gastronome Prue Leith later noted that 'not since Escoffier invented Peach Melba has a dish so fast become so famous'.

So when you stand with your yellow, creamy-filled baguette in front of the blue plaque adorning the wall of the Mayfair site where Spry plied her floral trade, spare a thought for her friend and culinary dynamo, Rosemary Hume, for it is to her that we owe so many great picnics.

 # Coronation Chicken

Try to use a decent curry powder but don't be tempted to turn up the heat, this is not about blowing your socks off but about soft background flavours. It works just as well in a crunchy baguette with shredded crispy lettuce if you want to eat it on the go.

Serves 8

- vegetable oil, for frying
- 5 cardamom pods
- 1 cinnamon stick
- 1 teaspoon black mustard seeds
- 1 litre good-quality chicken stock
- 4 chicken breasts, skin on
- 1 small onion, finely chopped
- 1 tablespoon medium hot curry powder
- 100ml red wine
- 1 bay leaf
- 1 tablespoon tomato purée
- juice of ½ lemon
- 4 apricot halves, finely chopped
- 300ml mayonnaise
- salt and freshly ground black pepper
- 100ml whipping cream
- a small handful of sultanas soaked in 20ml water
- 1 Little Gem lettuce, leaves separated

- Heat a little oil in a saucepan and add the cardamom pods, cinnamon stick and mustard seeds. Allow to sizzle for a few seconds then add the chicken stock. Bring to a gentle boil then add the chicken breasts. Simmer slowly for 20 minutes then remove from the heat and leave the liquid to cool. Once totally cold, cut the chicken into strips and set aside.

- Meanwhile, heat another saucepan with 1 tablespoon of vegetable oil and add the onion. Cook for about 3 minutes then add the curry powder, cook for a further 30 seconds then add the wine, bay leaf, tomato purée and lemon juice. Simmer very gently for 10 minutes then strain the sauce.

- Purée the apricots in a food processor then add to the mayonnaise. Pour in the curry sauce and combine. If it is too thick then add a little of the chicken poaching liquid. Beat well and season.

- Whip the cream into soft peaks and fold through the mayonnaise. Finally add the sultanas and chicken and mix thoroughly.

- Fill the Little Gem lettuce leaves with the chicken and serve.

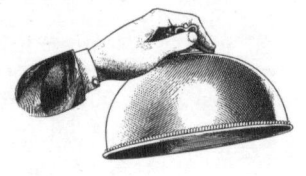

Chicken Marengo

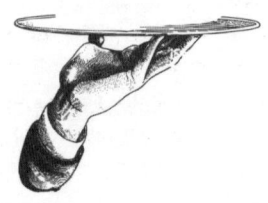

At first glance there are few things more unlikely to go together in a recipe than crayfish, chicken, eggs and cognac, but there are also times when culinary minds are pushed to the extremes of their creative knowledge and forced into a situation where needs must. The origin of Chicken Marengo is one of those times. Maybe it's the story of triumph over adversity that has given it a place in the hearts of gourmets or perhaps it is the combination of tender chicken, sweet tomatoes and crayfish punctuated by rich egg and salty olives (a late and very pleasing addition) that has struck a chord. In essence this is a simple one-pot dish with no frills, but all together it is a dish of wonder and drama.

According to legend, it came about like this. In the spring of 1800 Napoleon Bonaparte, newly installed as First Consul of France, had undertaken an invasion of the Austrian territories of northern Italy. His army had to cross the treacherous and unforgiving Alps and as a result his supply chain had been stretched perilously thin. Napoleon strongly believed that 'an army marches on its stomach' and in order to keep them all, and himself, well fed he had brought a large catering corps headed by a middle-aged Swiss-born chef named Dunand. We don't know his first name, but we know he was the son of the Prince of Condé's personal chef and that the Prince was one of France's great gourmets.

On 14 June the French army suffered a surprise attack at Marengo in Piedmont and for much of the day it looked as if it would be defeated. Clever generalship by Napoleon and the arrival of reserves in the nick of time secured a decisive victory, which Napoleon regarded as his greatest ever and which played no small part in his becoming Emperor four years later.

But as French troops fought tirelessly on the Piedmont plains, Chef Dunand faced a battle of a very different kind. He knew that his leader never ate before a battle but liked to feast immediately afterwards. With his supplies running low, he dispatched his aides to forage the local wilderness for anything they could find. They came back with a scrawny chicken, four tomatoes, a handful of eggs, a few small crayfish from the river and, some say, a frying pan. Dunand quickly dispatched the chicken with his sabre and set to braising it with a little garlic and the tomatoes. He served the crayfish and eggs as a garnish along with croutons made from the soldiers' dry bread.

Napoleon loved it. He loved it so much that he decreed it must be served after every battle for the rest of the campaign. Dunand tried to improve it whenever he had time, making it more 'classical' by adding brandy or eggs to the sauce or using lobster or other more luxurious ingredients. But Napoleon was superstitious, and he was adamant that the dish should always be served the way it had been on the evening of his great victory.

Time is a great leveller of legend and many keen-eyed researchers have questioned whether Dunand was even present at Marengo. Historians of the time didn't take much notice of who cooked the food that warring armies ate and some records suggest that Dunand was still in the employ of the Prince of Condé in 1800. However, most respected food authorities, including *Larousse Gastronomique* and *The Oxford Companion to Food*, credit Dunand and none casts the slightest doubt on the dish's association with the battle. Its place in history, and that of the small town outside Turin, are assured.

There is, however, another patriotic story that could easily go hand in hand with this one: when news of the great French victory reached Paris, one restaurateur, already renowned for his veal ragout, proudly renamed the dish Veal Marengo. Julia Child gives a recipe for this, suggesting that she regarded it as a 'classic' of French cuisine alongside its better-known poultry cousin.

Modern versions of Chicken Marengo have added olives, onions and mushrooms, but it remains a simple dish and, as with many great dishes, this is part of the reason for its longevity. Perhaps, like the battle-weary chef, our culinary creativity gets reined in on a busy weekday evening and the fact that chicken is now abundant (Dunand would have enjoyed the irony) and cheap makes it an appealing ingredient. Personally, I think we all love to imagine ourselves as little Napoleons in some way, and what better dish to come home to after a day fighting through the traffic than the great Chicken Marengo?

Chicken Marengo

This dish can turn a rainy weekday evening into a much brighter affair. It's hearty and warming and although Napoleon would never approve, I think prawns work just as well as crayfish, which can be a little tricky to get hold of unfrozen.

Serves 4

- 50g butter
- 1 tablespoon sunflower oil
- 1 medium-sized chicken, cut into 8 serving pieces (ask your butcher to do this 'to sauté')
- 4 banana shallots
- 50g plain flour
- 300ml dry white wine
- 150ml chicken stock
- 400g can chopped tomatoes
- 400g button mushrooms
- 2 tablespoons tomato purée
- 50ml brandy
- 2 garlic cloves, crushed
- a handful of freshly chopped parsley
- salt and salt and freshly ground black pepper
- 4 large, thick-cut slices of white bread
- 3 tablespoons olive oil
- 1 sprig of rosemary
- 300g cooked crayfish, peeled (prawns will do if you can't find crayfish)

- Preheat the oven to 180°C/Gas Mark 4. Melt the butter with the oil in a large, flameproof casserole dish. Add the chicken pieces when the butter starts to foam and cook until brown – this should take about 10–12 minutes. Remove the chicken and put on some kitchen paper.

- Add the shallots and cook for about 8 minutes until coloured then remove them and leave on kitchen paper. Drain off most of the fat from the casserole dish and add the flour and cook until lightly browned. Pour in the wine and stock then reduce the heat and gently simmer for about 10 minutes. Add the tomatoes, mushrooms, tomato purée, brandy, garlic, parsley (reserving some for the garnish) and salt and pepper to taste.

- Return the shallots and chicken to the casserole and increase the heat. Once it boils, cover and cook in the oven for 1 hour or until the chicken is almost tender.

- Cut the bread into small cubes and drizzle with the oil ensuring it is well coated. Finely chop the rosemary, sprinkle over the bread and bake at 180°C/Gas Mark 4 for 15 minutes or until the croutons are golden. Turn them a couple of times during cooking.

- Remove the casserole from the oven, stir in the crayfish or prawns and return to the oven for 10 minutes.

- Dish up on to four plates and garnish each serving with the reserved parsley and croutons.

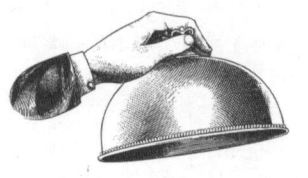

Kung Pao Chicken

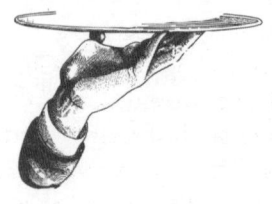

Even in this very modern world with all our technology and social networking there are still parts of the world that we, in the West, know terribly little about. There are new cuisines and new influences constantly being explored and plundered for ideas and inspiration for our inquisitive appetites. Most people's experience of Chinese food is from the super-fast and efficient delivery service we all have on our doorsteps. We may even have wandered through one of the many 'China Town' areas in one of the cities across this country and beyond. All are teeming with life and full of restaurants; all seem to serve a very similar selection of dishes and all seem to serve it in the same frantic manner, often with distinctly disinterested service. I am not a betting man but I would wager that every single one of the menus features a version of Kung Pao Chicken. It is a dish that encompasses all that is exciting about Chinese food – its mixture of pungent spiciness and tingling Szechuan flavours along with the texture of crispy peanuts and soft chicken is probably the most typical of all Chinese dishes. It represents all the different flavours and textures of all the different aspects of Chinese food in one small bowl of zingy tastiness.

The dish has its origins in the middle of the nineteenth century when China was nearing the end of its last imperial dynasty, the Qing Dynasty. China was a rebellious place and feudal lords were the order of the day. The clan of Jurchen Aisin Gioro had seized control from the previous Ming dynasty. Their rule would last into the twentieth century and would see the end of the old ways and a new republic emerge, eventually plunging China into the world of Mao Zedong and his hardline socialist ideals.

This was all some time away when in 1876 Ding Baozhen was appointed Governor of Szechuan Province.

It was an expected outcome for a man who had already shown his leadership skills as Head of Shandong Province and by achieving an outstanding result on the annual Royal Examination. Possibly his greatest achievement was in the reconstruction of one of China's greatest engineering projects, the irrigation infrastructure surrounding the Min River that runs through the heart of Szechuan. It allowed the area to once again become the most productive in the whole of China and eradicated the constant threat of flooding to the nearby towns and villages. Ding Baozhen was honoured by the erection of a statue in Dujiangyan City, which can still be seen today.

However, the Qing Dynasty was under constant feudal threat and the economic conditions in China as a whole were slowly deteriorating. People were hungry and food was in increasingly short supply. Quality was dropping and chefs, both at home and in the palaces of Szechuan, had to look to ways to spice their dishes up. The countryside of Szechuan has one great ingredient native to it, the mouth-numbing peppercorns that bear the name of the province. They create a sensation the Chinese call 'ma'. It is addictive and Ding Baozhen loved it. He was an astute man and often spent his time among the everyday people, sampling their food and listening to their stories. The spice of the peppercorns and the heat from chilli and plenty of garlic helped to mask the perhaps poorer qualities of some of the produce the people had at their disposal, but the dish had heart and power. Ding Baozhen would eat it often, usually with chicken but also with prawns. The dish was given the moniker Gōng Bǎo after Ding Baozhen's job title of palatial guardian and as a mark of respect for his earnest work in the region.

Ding Baozhen stepped down as Governor in 1886 but the dish stayed on and the cuisine of the region slowly gained international recognition. Its variety of cooking techniques coupled with intriguing but distinct ingredients had made it a destination for global food-lovers. As the Qing dynasty began to crumble it opened the gateways for foreign trading and post-Napoleonic Europe searched for new markets to conquer. It was inevitable that Europeans would fall in love with the food of Szechuan and in particular the glistening golden jewels of Gōng Bǎo chicken. Sadly they couldn't get their tongues around the name and little by little it became Kung Pao, or King Pow, or Kung Po, or any one of the hundred different ways you will see it on restaurant menus today.

As well as being one of Chinese cuisine's most enduring and endearing dishes, Kung Pao Chicken holds one other quite unique accolade. During Mao's Cultural Revolution the recipe was labelled as politically incorrect! So for nearly 40 years the dish became known as 'fast-fried chicken cubes' to avoid any reference to Ding Baozhen and his imperialistic era.

Our love affair with Kung Pao Chicken can be traced straight back to the very first Chinese restaurants that started to crop up in Britain in the 1950s. A post-war boom in the number of Chinese immigrants (fleeing from Mao) led to the number of Chinese living in Britain increasing from 3,000 to nearly half a million. The version we are served up today may lack some of the more straight-punching spiciness of its Szechuan ancestor but I think Ding would still recognize the tingling beauty of his beloved Kung Pao Chicken.

Kung Pao Chicken

The recipe here is my halfway house between old and new. Feel free to adapt and play but two things must happen. First try to get all the ingredients to the same size and second you **must** use Szechuan peppercorns. Enjoy!

Serves 4

- 2 boneless chicken breasts without skin
- 2 tablespoons peanut oil
- 3 dried red chillies, deseeded and cut into 5cm strips
- 1 teaspoon whole Szechuan peppercorns
- 5cm piece of fresh ginger, peeled and thinly sliced
- 3 garlic cloves, sliced thinly
- 4 large spring onions (cut the very green stalks off and discard. Cut remaining into 1cm pieces)
- a handful of roasted unsalted peanuts (or soak salted ones for 30 minutes before use)

For the marinade
- 2 teaspoons light soy sauce
- 2 teaspoons Shaoxing rice wine
- 2 teaspoons cornstarch

For the sauce
- 3 teaspoons caster sugar
- 1 teaspoon cornstarch
- 1 teaspoon dark soy sauce
- 1 teaspoon light soy sauce
- 1 teaspoon sesame oil

- Cut the chicken as evenly as possible into thin strips and then cut these into small cubes. Take your time and try to get the pieces of equal size. If you can get them to the size of a peanut you have done well. Place in a small bowl and mix in the marinade ingredients with 1 tablespoon water. Leave this for about 20 minutes if you can.

- Combine the sauce ingredients in a small bowl and mix thoroughly. The cornstarch may clump so do you best to mix it, but it will all even out in the wok later.

- Heat a wok over a high heat with the peanut oil. When the oil is hot add the chillies and Szechuan pepper and stir-fry briefly until they look just a little crispier, this will take less than a minute. The oil will have taken on some colour and be very fragrant. Take care not to burn the spices (you can remove the wok from the heat if necessary to prevent overheating).

- Quickly add the chicken and continue to fry over a high flame, stirring constantly. A minute or two after, add the ginger, garlic and spring onions and continue to stir-fry for a few minutes until things smell delicious and the meat is cooked through (test one of the larger pieces to make sure).

- Stir the sauce and add it to the wok, continuing to stir the contents of the wok quickly as they cook. As soon as the sauce has thickened and taken on a shiny appearance, add the peanuts, mix them through and serve.

- It's best served with rice to get all the sweet, sticky sauce. Any rice you like will do.

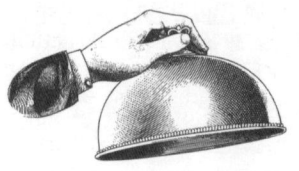

Chicken Kiev

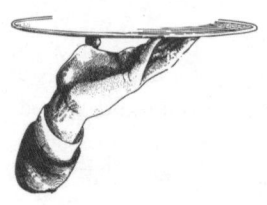

There was a time in the 1970s when a dinner party just wasn't worth going to if it didn't include the indulgence of chicken filled with garlic and butter, all covered in breadcrumbs, deep fried and served with thin fries. These days the bird used in a Kiev may not be chicken at all but pheasant or guinea fowl, with its filling anything from tarragon to hazelnuts. And it may share the name of Ukraine's capital city Kyiv, but it is about as authentically Eastern European as Sean Connery's accent in the Cold War blockbuster *The Hunt for Red October*.

However, there is a little science involved in understanding the heat transfer between the outer crust and the soft butter inside, so it is not surprising that its creation is credited to a man who eventually made his name through the application of science to food.

Nicolas Appert, born in 1749 in northeastern France, was many things: a brewer, a pickler and a confectioner. In the course of his varied career, he noticed that certain products could be manipulated under different conditions; sugar could be pulled and stretched, beer could be brewed – it was simple chemistry. Working as a chef in Paris, he wanted to find a way to stop the stuffing inside a chicken breast from burning or leaking, and he stumbled across the technique of using egg to seal the outer surface. It made the 'parcel' airtight and allowed the butter inside to melt slowly and then give a satisfying molten exit once cut. He called the dish *côtelettes de volaille*.

Now, in the middle of the eighteenth century France was enjoying a gastronomic boom. Elizabeth Petrovna, Empress of Russia from 1741 to 1762, loved everything about France; she sent her cooking staff to be trained in Paris and led the way in hiring the best French chefs to cook in Moscow and St Petersburg. Also, the French aristocratic way of life was under threat and would soon be under the guillotine, so it's easy to see why so many French chefs and French dishes made their way to Russia and became huge hits.

Côtelettes de volaille was one of these. It was soon on many restaurant menus and starting to be noticed in recipe books, newspapers and other publications. But then, 50 years later, world events intervened in its story. After the Russian Revolution of 1917 and the First World War, many people from battered parts of Europe fled to start a new life in the United States, but they hankered for the dishes they loved from their old homes. *Côtelettes de volaille* was soon being served in restaurants across the country, but someone realized that the name did not roll off the tongue, nor did *Tsiplenokovo Po-Kievski*, its Russian equivalent. Chicken Kiev did, though. It said just enough to appeal to the people it was targeted at, but was simple enough for others to remember. We know that in the 1930s Chicken Kiev was being sold in two Russian restaurants in Chicago, but it's more likely that the idea came from cynical restaurateurs in the New York area, eager to make a buck by tugging on the heartstrings of their new neighbours.

Nicolas Appert would be more celebrated for his culinary creation had the process used to create it not proved to be far more important. To finish our story, then, we must go back to France in the late eighteenth century and Napoleon's concern, documented elsewhere in this book, for feeding himself and his army only the best-quality French food. This created big supply problems, so the French government issued a challenge: whoever could invent a way to preserve food so that it could be transported thousands of kilometres without being ruined would receive 12,000 francs – roughly $40,000 in today's money.

Appert had been experimenting with this for some time; he found that if food was heated to a high enough temperature and cooked completely, then kept sealed in an airtight container, it would remain unspoilt for as long as three months. In 1810 he submitted his discovery to the Emperor, won the prize and in the same year described his work in his book, *The Art of Preserving Animal and Vegetable Substances*. As the idea quickly caught on, food became available in all sorts of vessels. And in 1979, almost 170 years later, there is a lovely example of events coming full circle when a certain British chain ventured into 'cook-chill' ready meals: yes, you guessed it, one of the first two dishes they chose for their new range was Chicken Kiev. Nicolas Appert would have approved.

 # Chicken Kiev

This version of the classic chicken dish is the work of the wonderful chef Silvena Rowe. It's a dish that requires a little attention to detail as the chicken must have a perfect seal or you will end up with butter all over the kitchen. Try not to double coat the chicken in the egg as it can make the dish a little soggy.

Serves 4

- 4 large chicken breasts, preferably with the wing bone still in
- salt and freshly ground black pepper
- 2 tablespoons plain flour
- 2 eggs, beaten
- 6 tablespoons homemade breadcrumbs
- vegetable oil, for frying

For the herb butter
- 200g butter, softened
- 1 teaspoon freshly chopped tarragon
- 1 teaspoon freshly chopped parsley
- 1 teaspoon freshly chopped chives
- 3 tablespoons lemon juice

- First make your herb butter. Put the butter, herbs and lemon juice in a small bowl and mix well. Shape the butter into four rolls about 5cm long and put in the fridge to chill.

- Remove the first thin joint of the wing from each chicken breast and slice the breast halfway down the middle with a very sharp knife so that it butterflies out. Lay each butterflied breast on a board and beat with a meat hammer (or rolling pin) between some clingfilm. Flatten the breasts out skin-side down. Season the chicken, put the butter inside each breast and roll up making sure to tuck the ends in. Secure with a toothpick.

- Put the flour, eggs and breadcrumbs in three separate bowls and roll the chicken first in the flour, then the egg and finally the breadcrumbs. Repeat for all four breasts.

- Heat your oil to 180°C, either in a large saucepan or a deep-fat fryer, and fry the chicken breasts two at a time and for no more than about 8 minutes. The breadcrumbs should be golden brown and cooked through. Alternatively, sauté the chicken in a saucepan with a little oil and butter for 5–6 minutes, turning in the pan to cook the chicken on all sides and then finish in a medium oven (180°C/Gas Mark 4) for 20 minutes.

- Serve with a green salad or straw-cut fries. I like mine with a simple potato salad of blanched potato and homemade mayonnaise dusted with a little paprika.

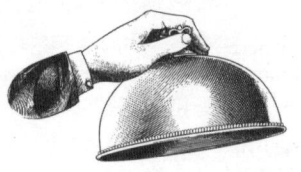

Sole Véronique

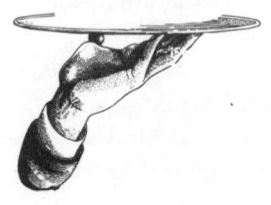

Any dish using either Dover or lemon sole conjures up something special, usually a night out at a glamorous restaurant. Often the fish is plated at the tableside with huge amounts of theatre and even more butter. By contrast, Sole Véronique is understated and restrained. Yes, it is one of the few dishes in the culinary world to include grapes and it also has a decadent amount of double cream, but overall it is a recipe with subtle nuances, the sweet juice from small Muscat grapes and the savouriness of Vermouth-infused cream gently blanketing the most delicately flavoured of the fish family.

Many new dishes are created through accident and circumstance, the most frequent being a shortage of ingredients. However, sometimes a chef heads to the larder with the sole purpose of conjuring up a bit of culinary wizardry. To make real magic happen takes a magician. And Auguste Escoffier wasn't just a magician, he was the greatest sorcerer of them all.

Escoffier began cooking in 1859, at the age of 13, at his uncle's restaurant in Nice. His innate ability and his passion for food took him all over France and later Europe. He was a pioneer of technique and organization, one of the first to restructure menus into the order that food was eaten, rather than serving a vast array of dishes all at once; and he's credited with being the first chef to present the 'à la carte' menu.

He turned up in London in 1889, when he and hotelier César Ritz were recruited by the impresario Richard D'Oyly Carte to help set up his latest venture, the Savoy Hotel. Everything about the Savoy was revolutionary: it had electric lifts, luxurious rooms with en suite bathrooms and hot and cold running water throughout. Escoffier set about creating a cuisine to match. However, the relationship between the three men soon soured. The chef and the manager were unceremoniously sacked amid accusations of fraud and bribery, only to land very much on their feet with new hotels of their own, first the self-named Ritz in Paris (1898) and then back in London with the Carlton (1899). It was as if nothing had changed. Escoffier was at the height of his powers and once again set the standard for London cuisine. When it came to knowing his audience there was no chef better.

Escoffier was ultimately a showman and a salesman. Both he and Ritz understood that half the battle of running a hotel or restaurant was footfall, getting people through the doors. They also knew that customers are a little like moths – they often make their choices based on the brightest light or the noisiest event. Escoffier had long been a fan of naming dishes after people and places – it was part of French culinary history going back to Napoleonic times and beyond. But for Sole Véronique he chose not a real person, but a theatrical characterization that was the talk of the town.

This was the time of comic operas. Almost 30 years earlier D'Oyly Carte had paved the way by producing the works of Gilbert and Sullivan; in 1903 London's 'big new show' was *Véronique*, an *opéra comique* by André Messager which, fortunately for a certain flatfish recipe, turned out to be the composer's most enduring creation. It first appeared in London at the Coronet Theatre in Notting Hill in its original French, but moved a year later to the Apollo on Shaftesbury Avenue, the heart of the capital's theatreland, where it would stay for a satisfying 496 performances.

Very much like today, the London theatre crowd liked to dine out before or after the performance and restaurants vied for their custom. Escoffier's menu was already popular, so when he cleverly tied it in with Messager's witty work by naming a light and delicate fish dish in its honour he immediately had another hit on his hands.

The recipe was published in Escoffier's *Guide Culinaire* and, like so many of his others, became famous wherever French cuisine was admired. By the middle of the twentieth century nearly every cookery school on the planet was using Escoffier's recipes to educate its pupils – and in the United States Sole Véronique was served to both Presidents Richard Nixon and Gerald Ford at White House dinners in the 1970s. I suspect its staying power comes largely from its being a simple way of dealing with a fish that can be tricky for the home cook to get right. Its pale complexion with light green dots of colour also makes it one of the most stunning-looking dishes in the seafood repertoire.

Sole Véronique

This recipe has been borrowed from the great British chef, Mark Sargeant. Cooking fish well is what marks a chef out for high accolades and there is none better at it than Mark. You will see there is nothing daunting or complicated about this dish and cooking it will get you one step closer to getting inside the culinary mind of Escoffier!

Serves 4

- 700g Dover or lemon sole fillets, skinned and trimmed (or 2 fillets per person)
- salt and freshly ground white pepper
- 400ml fish stock (or a good-quality fish stock cube dissolved in 400ml water)
- 100ml vermouth, preferably Noilly Pratt
- 300ml double cream
- 1 egg yolk
- 40 seedless white grapes (Muscat grapes are best), peeled and halved

- Preheat the grill to high. Season the fish and roll the fillets. This gives a better texture as they can be quite thin. Put them in a wide saucepan with a tight-fitting lid and pour in the stock and vermouth. Poach the fillets for 3–4 minutes. Remove them from the liquid and keep warm under some baking parchment.

- Reduce the poaching liquid down to 4–5 tablespoons in volume and then away from the heat add the cream (reserving about a tablespoon). Return to the heat and allow the mixture to thicken. It will come down to about two-thirds of the original volume and should coat a spoon like thin custard.

- Meanwhile, mix the egg yolk and the remaining cream in a bain-marie until the mixture froths and thickens.

- Add the grapes to the sauce and pour in the egg mixture. Whisk it quickly then pour this over the fish fillets (drained of any resting residue) and place under the hot grill. Let the sauce glaze slightly for about 1 minute then serve with some fresh green vegetables – I like green beans but any will do.

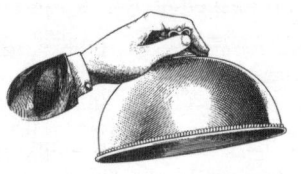

Choron Sauce

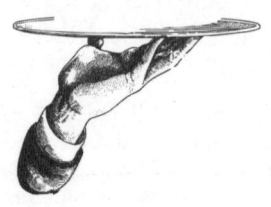

Choron Sauce itself is a little-used side note to the much more popular béarnaise, but its story is remarkable. It comes in two parts: the first is a pretty unextraordinary tale of gastronomic wizardry by a great chef working in a great kitchen at a great time in Paris's history, but the second is something different altogether. So if you are sitting comfortably, let's begin…

In 1836, one of the grandest restaurants in Paris was the newly opened Pavillon Henri IV. For the opening, chef Jean-Louis-François Collinet had created a variation on the classic melted-butter-and-egg-yolk hollandaise sauce by infusing it with tarragon and shallots. He named it béarnaise, after the province where King Henri IV, namesake of the restaurant, was born.

End of part one. For part two, we move forward 25 years to 1861, a time when arguably the finest of many fine restaurants in Paris was Le Voisin. One of its waiters was a bright young man called César Ritz, whom you will come across elsewhere in this book; its head chef was Alexandre Choron. It was he who took Collinet's creation and replaced the tarragon with a rich tomato concasse; the result was a vibrant pink sauce that not only looked great on either fish or meat, but also added a refreshing sweetness to finish off a dish.

Things went well at Voisin over the next few years, but the same couldn't be said for the rest of France. The reign of Napoleon III ended unceremoniously with defeat in the Franco-Prussian War and, despite some brave battles throughout the country, on 19 September 1870 the Prussian army parked itself outside Paris and laid siege to the city.

By Christmas all supply lines in and out of the capital were static. Butchers were doing a roaring trade, charging three francs each for rats and a costly ten francs for a tasty moggy. The Seine was completely stripped of fish and even a can of sardines would set you back five francs. For the starving Parisian it was necessary protein, but for those more used to caviar and fresh lobster this was a deeply unsettling period.

With Christmas approaching and people wanting to feast, Choron saw an opportunity. A frequent visitor to the Jardin d'Acclimatation, a zoo in the northern part of the city, he saw that the animals were starving too. Their food had long since been used up to feed the people and many animals were being shipped out to other zoos or set free to fend for themselves. This worked perfectly well for smaller mammals or birds, but for the large beasts it was hardly an adequate solution. So Choron bought all of them: elephants, bears, wolves, kangaroos and camels. He took them home, butchered them into recognizable joints and put them in his larder. He then set about designing a menu based around cuts of bear and elephant, matching the meat to his wide repertoire of sauces, including the tomato-purée-infused béarnaise that would soon bear his name.

The meal served at Le Voisin on Christmas Day 1870, the 99th day of the siege, has become the stuff of legend. The six-course menu began with a donkey's head terrine, skipped lightly through an elephant consommé, then into a delightful trio of roast camel, kangaroo stew and bear's ribs in a pepper sauce. For most people that would have been enough, but remember this was nineteenth-century Paris – what followed was the pièce de résistance: a whole haunch of wolf served with a reduced deer-stock sauce along with a witty display of slowly roasted cat, flanked by spit-roasted rat. This lavish main course came with a watercress salad, a little antelope and truffle terrine, some mushrooms in red wine and a few peas. Choron closed the show with a jam rice pudding and some Gruyère cheese – all washed down, of course, with the finest French wines available.

Choron continued to served his exotic menus throughout the siege, but when it ended on 28 January 1871 Paris's era of gluttonous indulgence was at an end. France's Third Republic took a more egalitarian view on food, resulting in a mass evacuation of chefs and aristocracy. Many headed for England and America, taking their knowledge and skills with them and thus igniting our own culinary revolutions. And so a light pink tomato béarnaise sauce was passed from chef to chef along with a tale of culinary resourcefulness like no other. Little is known about Choron after this point and Le Voisin eventually closed, leaving only the memory of a terrible time and a menu of incredible dark delights, with one light pink sauce that goes remarkably well with both meat and fish. Not a bad legacy after all.

Choron Sauce

This is a sauce that goes well with both steak and a nice firm fish like sea bass. The shallot and tomato mixture must be left to cool before adding the eggs or they will cook in the heat. If this happens there is no way back and you must start again.

Serves 4

- 3 tablespoons white wine vinegar
- 3 tablespoons white wine
- 10 black peppercorns, lightly crushed
- 2 tablespoons shallots, finely chopped
- 1 teaspoon finely chopped tarragon leaves
- 1 tablespoon tomato purée
- 3 free-range egg yolks
- 200g butter, melted
- salt and freshly ground black pepper
- 1 tablespoon finely chopped flatleaf parsley

- Put the white wine vinegar, white wine, black peppercorns, shallots and tarragon into a stainless steel saucepan and bring to the boil. Reduce the heat and simmer until the liquid in the pan has reduced to about 1 tablespoon in volume.

- Add the tomato purée and 1 tablespoon water to the pan and whisk to combine. Beat in the egg yolks, whisking for 3–4 minutes over a low heat or until frothy. Gradually pour in the butter in a thin, steady stream, whisking continuously until all of the butter has been incorporated and the sauce is thickened. Season to taste with salt and freshly ground black pepper, then strain the sauce through a fine sieve.

- Discard the solids left behind in the sieve. Keep the sauce warm until ready to serve. Stir the parsley into the sauce just before serving.

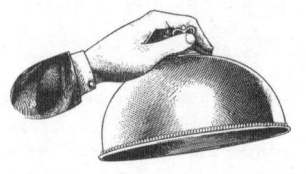

Cod Mornay

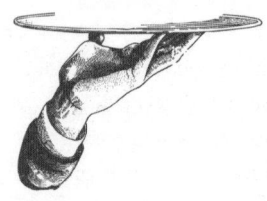

For a dish as simple as white fish covered in milk sauce with the addition of a handful of tangy hard cheese, Cod Mornay has a surprising number of – disputed – claims to its creation. It represents the evolution of French cookery over a period of some three hundred years and the best way to understand it is to try to trace the culinary footsteps that made it what it is.

Saucing has always been vital to French cookery. Pouring a liquid over a dry, often cured piece of meat or fish could turn the unpalatable into something that could keep both body and spirits alive. It was Marie-Antoine Carême who in the nineteenth century first catalogued the four main classifications of sauces: espagnole (aka brown sauce), velouté, béchamel and allemande (a velouté thickened with egg and a touch of lemon). But we need to look further back to see who was responsible for the first béchamel.

Sometime in the seventeenth century, the Marquis Louis de Béchamel, chief steward to King Louis XIV and lover of good food, was, according to legend, staring at some overcooked cod. Thinking that a meaty velouté was perhaps not the perfect companion, he replaced the stock with warm milk infused with cloves and pepper. End of story, you might think, but no: there is evidence of similar white sauces appearing in various culinary repertoires around this time. One of those belonged to Duke Philippe de Mornay, Governor of Saumur, who is credited with a number of key kitchen developments – not only the sauce that bears his name, but Sauce Chasseur, Sauce Lyonnaise and Sauce Porto. While it is certainly believable that these two wealthy gourmets had large and inventive kitchens to cater for their every whim, the reality is that there is no proof of the foodie credentials of either of them.

The first recorded béchamel sauce appears in *Le Cuisinier François*, the first great tome of French gastronomy. It was assembled by François Pierre de la Varenne, a Burgundian chef, and published in 1651. La Varenne had spent many years working for the Marquis d'Uxelles (after whom he named his preparation of mushrooms) and had helped move French food away from the heavy spicing of the Middle Ages and towards the use of fresh herbs, new vegetables and fresh fish. He was one of the first to propose cooking vegetables separately: he suggested preparing fresh asparagus by lightly poaching and serving simply with a butter emulsion; and he had ideas for exciting new products such as cauliflower, peas, cucumber and artichoke.

The impact of La Varenne's work was like a thunderbolt, a reboot in the culinary software. It introduced ideas, terms and techniques that are standard today: bouquet garni, egg-white clarification, even an early hollandaise are down to La Varenne. Most of all he took the world to the new frontier of lighter sauces based on butter and flour. *Le Cuisinier François* was a huge success internationally and became the first cookbook translated into English from French.

It is perfectly credible, despite a lack of evidence, that when La Varenne was working on basic white sauces he would remember the version talked about by Béchamel. In a book containing several thousand recipes, naming a sauce after the Marquis was no more than the flick of a pen. Little did he know that some two hundred years later Carême would declare the sauce a fundamental building block of French cuisine and use it to push dishes higher into the gastronomic stratosphere.

So how did grated cheese get involved? To find the answer we have to jump to the heady world of late-nineteenth-century Paris café society, where people lived for lunch and dinner in places like Restaurant Vefour and Le Durand, at the corner of Place de la Madeleine and Rue Royale. The chef in charge at Le Durand was Joseph Voiron, whose sauces were clean and light in the modern style. It was he who made the now blindingly obvious step of adding grated cheese to his béchamel. He must have seen how the cheese melted and gave way to the sauce, enriching it and giving it a cutting edge to work well with any firm white fish. *Larousse Gastronomique* says that the sauce's name has nothing to do with the grand old Governor of Saumur but is a tribute to Joseph's eldest son and fellow chef, Mornay.

So Sauce Mornay has passed through the hands of some of the greatest chefs ever to have graced this planet and has culminated in a father handing immortality to his son. Surely the perfect end to a recipe that has its origins in the very beginnings of French gastronomy.

Cod Mornay Fishcakes

Feel free to couple the sauce with a simple grilled piece of cod, the thicker the better, and grill the skin until it is super crispy if you wish. History points to Gruyère cheese being used in a classic Mornay – Cheddar can be a little too powerful.

Serves 4

- 450g Icelandic cod, skinned
- 2 bay leaves
- 150ml milk
- 350g Maris Piper potatoes, cooked
- ½ teaspoon finely grated lemon zest
- 1 tablespoon freshly chopped flatleaf parsley
- 1 tablespoon finely chopped chives
- salt and freshly ground black pepper
- 100g white breadcrumbs, preferably slightly stale
- 1 egg, beaten
- vegetable oil, for shallow-frying

For the mornay sauce
- 30g butter
- 30g plain flour, plus extra for dusting
- 500ml milk
- pinch of nutmeg
- salt and freshly ground white pepper
- 3 egg yolks
- 50ml double cream
- 100g Gruyère cheese, finely grated

- Put the cod in a shallow frying pan with the bay leaves and cover with the milk and 150ml water. Cover with a lid and gently bring to the boil. Reduce the heat to an almost imperceptible simmer and cook for 3–4 minutes. Remove from the heat and leave to cool, still covered, for about 10 minutes.

- Using a slotted spoon or fish slice gently remove the fish from the milk. Pass the cooked potatoes through a potato ricer leaving a light, fluffy mash. Away from the heat add the lemon zest, parsley and chives. Season well, making sure to taste as you go. Grind some pepper over the fish and flake into the potatoes in big chunks. If the mixture is a little dry add a teaspoon of milk. Using your hands gently combine the potato and fish, trying not to break the fish up too much. Set the fishcakes aside to cool.

- Flour a board and spread the breadcrumbs out on a plate. Roll the fishcakes in the flour and shape into cakes about 2–3cm thick. Dip each one in the egg and then the breadcrumbs ensuring all sides are lightly covered. Put on a plate and chill in the fridge for at least 30 minutes.

- To make the sauce, melt the butter in a heavy-based saucepan over a low heat and add the flour, whisking for about 2–3 minutes. Slowly pour in the milk, whisking continuously and bring to the boil. When it begins to boil, reduce the heat and simmer gently, stirring frequently, for about 10 minutes. Season with the nutmeg, salt and white pepper. Mix the egg yolks and cream in a bowl then pour the mixture into the sauce and allow it to bubble for 1 minute, whisking continuously. Remove from the heat and add the cheese. Stir until melted.

- Heat the vegetable oil in a shallow frying pan. Test it with a breadcrumb to see if it browns in about 30 seconds. When it does, fry the fishcakes on both sides until the breadcrumbs are golden and crispy.

- To serve, place the fishcakes on four plates and cover generously with the Mornay Sauce. Garnish with watercress and a wedge of lemon.

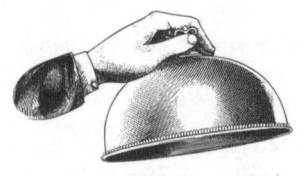

Oysters Rockefeller

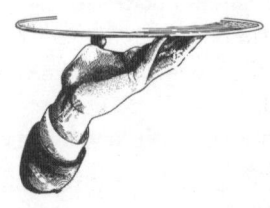

Jonathan Swift's famous line 'He was a bold man that first ate an oyster' sums up most people's view. Either they are free food, found abundantly in local waters and nothing to get excited about, or they are something alien to be viewed with suspicion. The British were largely unfamiliar with them until the Roman occupation. The Romans loved them; archaeologists and construction workers can testify to vast quantities of shells being found under nearly every road they built, and there is evidence that oysters were farmed at Whitstable in Kent up to 2,000 years ago. They were normally eaten raw, out of the half shell, so you can see how a marching army would have snacked and discarded the debris. Yet now oysters populate the finest restaurants in the world.

Like so many other great dishes, Oysters Rockefeller was born out of creative need and the throbbing beat of a hungry dining room. In about 1840 French-trained chef Antoine Alciatore abandoned New York and headed south to seek his culinary fortune. He landed in the melting pot of Louisiana, a state with a heavy European influence and an intoxicating obsession with voodoo. The people just happened to speak French, too, and Antoine opened a restaurant in the French Quarter which he called simply Antoine's. Its menu mixed Creole cuisine with classics from his time working in Marseilles. Everyone adored it and Antoine quickly found himself running the city's hottest eatery. He also began collecting and serving some of the best wines in the world, a tradition that continues today despite Hurricane Katrina's cataclysmic attack on the cellars in 2005.

By the time Antoine handed the reins to his son Jules in around 1880, the house speciality was snails, served in various different ways, slowly braised with garlic and herbs or with a spicy tomato sauce. Then, one night in 1899, Jules had been struggling with his supplier. The restaurant was full, there simply weren't enough snails to go around and he needed a hot starter for his customers. He looked in the larder and saw oysters. Oysters were abundant in the region and had long formed part of the everyday diet of the southern American diner, but there still was only one way to serve them – raw. Jules decided to change that. He blended herbs and shallots, threw in some breadcrumbs, then coated the oysters and put them under his grill. Quick, simple, stunning to look at and ever so filling. So hefty in fact that one diner declared the dish 'richer than Rockefeller himself'.

Another version of the story says that the green of the sauce reminded Jules of 'greenbacks' – banknotes – and he wanted a name that would signify 'the richest in the world'. Either way, the name Rockefeller was ideal, because at the time John D Rockefeller was not just rich, he was the richest man on the planet. His aggressive industrial strategy had allowed him and his company Standard Oil to dominate America's supply of oil. Surviving the usual boom and bust cycles of the economy, he had amassed a personal fortune close to ten billion dollars. The dish was the perfect tribute to the man and the reputation of oysters duly soared through the roof. Instead of being the free food anyone could eat, they became the hors d'oeuvre of choice of rich businessmen and bankers keen to buy into the American dream that Rockefeller represented.

Before this, very few places had served cooked oysters and word quickly spread about this vibrant green hit of pure seashore flavours. The shells provided a savoury note of a hot summer's beach which, coupled with the umami-rich oyster and the green herby crunch of the breadcrumb, brought more and more gourmet travellers to Antoine's to sample its trademark dish. Visiting presidents and film stars tucked into it. However, try as they might, they couldn't get their hands on the recipe. Jules trusted no one; he kept the secret close to his heart and never wrote it down, passing it on to his family orally. Other restaurants served the Rockefeller but only one place served *the* Rockefeller.

For Jules' imitators, the biggest bone of contention was the greenness of the sauce. Even a laboratory analysis in the 1980s failed to solved the problem. Spinach can easily be used to create the colour but every chef, past and present, at Antoine's has denied that Oysters Rockefeller contains spinach. Don't despair, though, as thankfully Antoine's is still with us, the oldest family-run restaurant in America. You can sample its most famous creation for yourself and have a guess at the recipe. Overleaf is my stab at it.

Oysters Rockefeller

Make sure you get a proper knife for opening up your oysters otherwise you will either lose your blade or worse still one of your fingers! Oysters are around all year but it's better to avoid the summer months in Britain when they are spawning as they can be a bit milky.

Serves 3–4

- 6 small fresh oysters on the half shell
- 1 tablespoon butter
- a handful of fresh spinach leaves
- 1 tablespoon chopped shallot
- ½ tablespoon finely chopped parsley, plus extra to serve
- 1 tablespoon homemade breadcrumbs
- Tabasco sauce, to taste
- dash of aniseed liqueur
- pinch of sea salt
- rock salt
- lemon wedges, to garnish

- Open the oysters carefully using an oyster knife. Hold the shell in a tea towel and make sure your hands don't slip. Empty the oysters into a bowl with the juice from inside the shell.

- Melt the butter in a saucepan and add the spinach, shallot and parsley. Cook for a minute until the spinach has wilted only slightly then toss in the breadcrumbs, Tabasco, aniseed liqueur and salt. Cook for a further 10 minutes until the breadcrumbs are nicely toasted. Tip the mixture into a food processor and blitz until smooth.

- Preheat the grill then put the oyster shells on a baking tray. Steady the shells using little piles of rock salt underneath. Put an oyster in each shell, moisten with a little oyster liquor, then cover each one in an equal amount of green sauce, spreading it to cover the oyster.

- Grill the oysters until they are just cooked and the sauce is bubbling – keep an eye on them as they won't take long.

- Serve with some more parsley and a wedge of lemon to squeeze over.

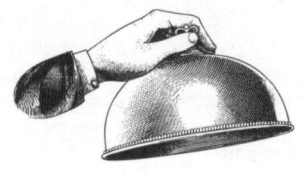

Lobster
Thermidor

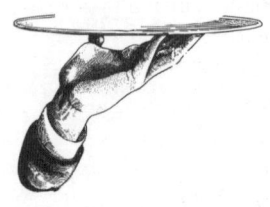

Lobster Thermidor has it all. Not only does it showcase one of the most luxurious ingredients in any chef's larder, but it combines it with some of the richest: cheese, cream, eggs and alcohol. This dish would be delicious served in a plain white bowl, but pile it back into that magnificent lobster shell and it's a feast for the eyes, nose and taste buds. The warming heat of that bright red armour adding the aroma of a hot beach just as it arrives at your table – heavenly! And to top it off it has the coolest name: Thermidor.

As scholars of history will know, the French Revolutionaries did away with months called after boring things like Roman gods, emperors or numbers and introduced names to do with – the weather. Thermidor referred to the heat of summer and it became famous for one of the last violent events of the Revolution. Known as the Thermidorian Reaction because it took place on 9 Thermidor Year 2 (27 July 1794), it saw the great revolutionary leader Maximilien Robespierre denounced, arrested and declared an outlaw. He was parted from his head the very next day.

At times like this it is usual for social commentators to put pen to paper, but in France too many heads were missing for people to be comfortable about exercising their creative freedom. It was almost a hundred years before the playwright Victorien Sardou portrayed the Revolution in a theatrical context. His play *Thermidor* tells the story of a young actor who infiltrates the powerful Committee for Public Safety and saves potential victims by burning their files.

Sardou had already made a name for himself, so any new work of his was hotly anticipated. When it was announced that *Thermidor* was to be staged for the first time at La Comédie Française in Paris on 24 January 1894, Sardou fever gripped the capital; critics called it the artistic event of the season. And in nearby Rue Saint Denis, restaurants prepared to fight for the pre- and post-theatre clientele. The one that rose most spectacularly to the occasion was Chez Marie, whose 'specials' board contained just three words – 'Tonight Lobster Thermidor!'

Chez Marie's creation was almost certainly inspired by the signature dish of Charles Ranhofer, head chef at Delmonico's restaurant in New York. His version consisted of lobsters covered in a sauce of cream, Madeira and cayenne, all enriched with egg. It was named initially after a sea captain called Ben Wenberg, who had allegedly introduced it to Delmonico's on his return from a trip to Cuba. The two men subsequently fell out and Ranhofer took the dish off the menu, but so many customers asked for it that he returned it, using an anagram of the name. Lobster Newberg was born, its fame spread and it may already have been on the menu at Chez Marie when the chefs created their new 'special'. Proud Frenchmen that they were, in order to make their dish different from its American relative, they used mustard instead of cayenne and cognac instead of Madeira.

Sardou's play and Marie's lobster dish were launched on the unsuspecting public together. Now it doesn't take a *New York Times* critic to tell you which fared better. *Thermidor*'s small audience took offence at its anti-government storyline: on the second night they were so incensed that a riot was narrowly avoided and the play was immediately banned from being performed in any state-funded venue. It had a second run in 1896, but again the reception was lacklustre. Thus the theatrical *Thermidor* was firmly consigned to our artistic past. But in terms of lobster, it was an instant hit.

Despite using the most high-end ingredients, its preparation, once practised, is relatively simple. Chefs from all over Paris popped this little gem into their culinary armoury and took it with them as they travelled the world; at the same time, with France enjoying its Belle Époque, many visitors stopped off to sample the fine wines and food, then began to demand them back home. In America, it quickly became the way to enjoy lobster if you were in a decadent frame of mind and it gained wider currency when Julia Child published a recipe in the 1960s. And in a neat example of history coming full circle, it was a classic of the El Floridita club in Havana: in the days before the 1959 revolution, Cuba was a playground for the wealthy, whose lasting legacy was their taste for fancy French food.

What's remarkable today is the power the name still holds. Seeing Lobster Thermidor on the menu is a sign that it's a special night, a momentous food night, a night when anything could happen. It brings to life those turbulent times of Robespierre and his co-revolutionaries. Just don't lose your head over it!

 # Lobster Thermidor

This is one of the most iconic seafood dishes. Rich and potent, it makes for a grand dinner party. If you can't find Gruyère cheese then a nice tangy Cheddar will be just fine, something like Lincolnshire Poacher would work well.

Serves 2

- 1 x 750g lobster, cooked
- 20g Gruyère cheese, grated
- salt and freshly ground black pepper

For the sauce
- 30g butter
- 1 shallot, finely chopped
- 30ml brandy
- 250ml fresh fish stock
- 55ml white wine
- 100ml double cream
- 1 teaspoon English mustard
- juice of ½ lemon
- 2 tablespoons freshly chopped parsley

- Preheat the grill to high. The lobster will come whole from your fishmonger so you need to cut it in half and take out any meat from the head end and the tail and set aside. Try to do this so you get nice big pieces. Then clean out any very dark stuff from the shell – it's not dangerous just unpleasant. Remove the meat from the claws, again take it slowly and try to get the meat out in one big piece. This dish is all in the presentation.

- To make the sauce, melt the butter in a saucepan until it is foaming, add the shallot and cook gently until it is soft with no colour. Add the brandy and burn off any alcohol (mind your eyebrows!). Add the fish stock, white wine and double cream and bring to the boil. Simmer gently until the sauce has reduced by half and thickened. Add the mustard, lemon juice and parsley.

- Place the lobster meat back in the shell and pour over the sauce. Sprinkle with the cheese, season and place under the hot grill until golden brown.

- Serve immediately with a big bowl of straw-cut fries or a crunchy Little Gem salad dressed simply in olive oil and lemon juice.

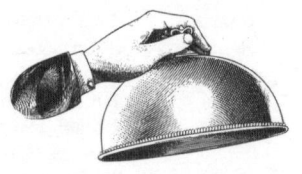

Omelette
Arnold Bennett

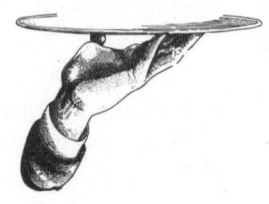

Certain ingredients are natural bedfellows. Strawberries and cream, lamb and mint, even pork and apples: their flavours help bring out the best in each other. Food scientists can probably explain how and why, but the rest of us just know that they do and let the results speak for themselves. Smoked fish and eggs are two such ingredients, rich yellow yolk flowing over the firm fishy flesh like a savoury blanket. This powerful combination has hearty breakfast written all over it, but the real joy of any good breakfast dish is having it at another time; for a dish to become elevated to the realm of classic it has to have a life beyond any particular mealtime.

Classic dishes don't get any more quintessentially British than the Omelette Arnold Bennett. Its story combines one of London's great hotels with one of England's most respected and prolific writers. However, before we get to Mr Bennett, let's quickly put the omelette in perspective. Although now known as a French dish it was probably born a little further east, where baked egg recipes were recorded as far back as the Middle Ages; a variation may even have been cooked in ancient Persia 2,500 years ago. Omelettes spread to Italy, Spain and France simultaneously as trade routes evolved and their first notable appearances in France came in about the sixteenth century. When Napoleon's armies swept through southern France at the end of the eighteenth century he fed them a giant omelette made by an innkeeper in the tiny town of Bessières, just outside Toulouse. It proved such a satisfying meal that he repeated it on later campaigns and in different towns. To this day Bessières annually holds a giant Easter omelette festival in Napoleon's honour.

Now let's jump forward 130 years or so and travel 900 kilometres to London, suffering in the aftermath of the

First World War and in the grip of the Great Depression. At the Savoy Hotel, Auguste Escoffier (the creator of a number of the recipes in this book) was a distant memory and its restaurants, although still home to the rich and famous, had lost much of their showbiz sparkle. For the first time in the hotel's history, the money men were looking at ways to seek out new clientele, some innovative ideas were needed. So when Arnold Bennett made it known that he was basing his latest novel, *Imperial Palace*, on the Savoy it made perfect sense for him to stay in residence while he wrote.

Bennett had set a previous novel, *The Grand Babylon Hotel*, in the Savoy, but now he wanted to study the hotel in great detail and draw authentic characters from actual serving members of staff. The Savoy saw its chance and made him feel very welcome. He would eat all his meals in the restaurant and grill while scrupulously observing the inner workings of the hotel. It was during one such working breakfast that Bennett, feeling particularly hungry, asked the waiter for an omelette with a little more substance than usual. So on that day in 1930 the first Omelette Arnold Bennett was created. The author loved it and ordered it frequently during his three-month stay and beyond.

The chef responsible, Jean Baptiste Virlogeux, went on to achieve more greatness at the Dorchester and became famous during the Second World War for his innovative ways of coping with rationing to maintain the high standards at the hotel. Bennett based the character of Rocco, the chef in *Imperial Palace*, on Virlogeux, describing him as a 'suave and stately gentleman' with 'an inordinately long brown silky moustache'.

Imperial Palace suffers from a rather heavy literary style and lacklustre plot; it was not the smash hit everyone hoped for. But it was highly regarded for the detail in which it captured life in a grand hotel. Bennett's work is not much studied these days and in some ways feels rather out of date. The omelette that bears his name has fared better – I suspect for exactly the same reasons his writing hasn't. It too feels old-fashioned and as a result chimes with food memories from a bygone era. History doesn't record exactly when Omelette Arnold Bennett was given its name, but its fame spread by word of mouth and soon featured on restaurant menus on both sides of the Atlantic. The Savoy still serves it every day. Its construction can be a little fiddly, but when executed correctly it is one of the great fish dishes of the world.

Omelette Arnold Bennett

Everyone must make this at least once in their lives. It's a classic café dish and you can't help feeling like the resident of a grand hotel as you tuck in. Be warned – it's very filling so leave time for a snooze afterwards.

Serves 4

- 600ml milk
- 2 cloves
- 2 bay leaves
- a few parsley stalks
- 1 medium-sized onion, chopped
- 400g smoked haddock
- 8 eggs, plus 4 egg yolks
- 75g butter
- 25g plain flour
- 50g Parmesan cheese, grated
- 4 teaspoons freshly chopped flatleaf parsley

- Heat the milk in a saucepan with the cloves, bay leaves, parsley stalks and the chopped onion. Bring to the boil then remove from the heat and set aside for 25 minutes to infuse.

- Turn the heat back on and bring the milk to a gentle simmer and carefully put the smoked haddock into it. Remove from the heat and allow the fish to cook in the milk as the milk cools.

- Whisk the whole eggs in a bowl. Once the fish is cool enough to handle, remove it from the milk and flake it into a separate bowl, strain the milk into a saucepan and warm slowly.

- In a separate pan melt a third of the butter, stir in the flour and cook for a few minutes – the flour needs to cook out and release its starch to make your sauce smooth. Gently pour in the warm milk and whisk quickly. Keep over a low heat for about 5 minutes until the sauce is thick and smooth. Remove from the heat and set aside.

- Divide the remaining butter between four blini pans or one large skillet depending on how you wish to serve the omelette. Add the eggs and cook them in the butter until they are just cooked at the bottom but liquid on top. Add the flaked smoked haddock and sprinkle over the Parmesan. Now add the egg yolks to the béchamel sauce and combine, then pour over the fish in the pan(s). Place the pan(s) under a hot grill and to finish cooking the eggs and allow the top to glaze.

- Serve in the blini pans or cut slices from the one pan and sprinkle with the parsley.

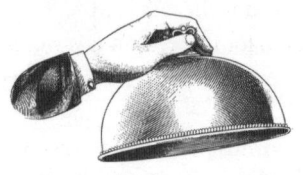

Woolton Pie

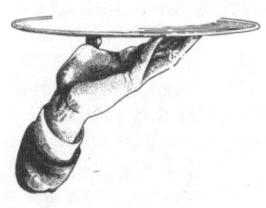

Woolton Pie, Woolton Pie: it doesn't matter how many times you say it, it really doesn't conjure up fond memories for most people. In essence it was, and is, a mixed vegetable pie. It is humble, it is very British and, like many unsung heroes of the twentieth century, it helped win a war. So for this reason it is worth celebrating.

When, in 1939, Europe was plunged into conflict for the second time in little more than two decades, much of British food production was immediately diverted towards feeding British troops. Importing food became much more difficult, too, leaving a nation staring at an increasingly bare store cupboard. But necessity is the mother of invention and times of adversity have always brought creative people to the fore.

It was with the pressing need to ensure there was enough for all that the British government founded the Ministry of Food and tasked it with the smooth and fair running of the rationing system. By 1940 the man in charge was Frederick Marquis, 1st Earl of Woolton. A former head of Lewis's department store in Liverpool, he knew all about giving the market what it wanted. But rationing allowed each civilian only one fresh egg a week, 50g of butter, 100g of meat and bacon and 50g of cheese. Sugar, tea and milk were also restricted. If people were to take on these new austerity plans, Woolton would have to help the medicine go down with some positive campaigning.

The one thing Britain had in plenty was vegetables and the nation had already been urged to 'dig for victory'. Every spare plot of land – parks, tennis courts, even the moat at the Tower of London – was used to grow vegetables. But how could the Ministry of Food keep people enthusiastic about their limited charms?

Woolton had two weapons up his sleeve. First he enlisted Elsie and Doris Waters, the country's foremost music-hall stars, to sing about the virtues of Potato Pete and Dr Carrot. Through cinema newsreels and the radio waves people would be entertained by songs such as:

> *And when your back aches laugh with glee*
> *And keep on diggin'.*
> *Till we give our foes a wiggin'.*
> *Dig! Dig! Dig! to Victory!*

There were rhymes and 'food flashes' about our great wartime allies, the potato and carrot. Dr Carrot would always be seen carrying his bag of vitamin A and Potato Pete would gently remind us that he didn't need a valuable ship to arrive at our grocers. Sweet things were particularly scarce and Woolton even managed to convince children that carrots were a good substitute. Any man who can get kids to eat a carrot on a stick instead of an ice cream deserves all the accolades we can throw at him!

The second of Woolton's secret weapons was the creative culinary mind of François Latry, head chef of the Savoy Hotel. Helped by a team of home economists and chefs who created and tested dishes with the few ingredients that were in good supply, Latry set to work designing something that was tasty, healthy and easy to cook.

Enlisting Latry gave the recipes a sense of professionalism: after all, here was a man used to serving royalty and superstars. What he came up with was a mixture of diced potato, cauliflower, swede, carrots and spring onions cooked in a little water with oatmeal and vegetable extract, then topped with wheatmeal pastry or potato slices. It was rudimentary to say the least, but it did the job. Now it just needed selling.

Woolton went on the offensive. Wherever he went, he would order the vegetable pie that bore his name. Cheap communal eating places called British Restaurants were formed; all served Woolton Pie along with other more protein-rich foods. Woolton's voice filled the radio airwaves, extolling the joys of his pie, and posters abounded advising everyone to eat their vegetables. Slowly but surely he persuaded people that this was good, healthy food.

Rationing continued until 1954, some nine years after the war had finished. So it is no surprise that, as soon as they could, people moved away from Woolton Pie and similar wartime dishes. These days they are consigned to the recipe books of history, but the role they played in keeping a nation fed should not be underestimated. In a modern world where we face pressures to eat our daily intake of fruit and vegetables, it is worth remembering the man who used his gift for publicity to make carrots and potatoes fun. Despite all the restrictions, there is no doubt that we ate more healthily 70 years ago than we do today.

Woolton Pie

This is a slice of pure wartime history and was part of a huge effort by the British people to win the war in Europe, but remember this pie was created with the purpose of filling you up so it is pretty hefty to eat. Also in times of peace you may wish to add some softer vegetables like peas or even a layer of spinach under the traditional pastry topping to give it a little more colour. I love to go over my potato ration and put mash on the top instead of pastry but feel free to use pastry if you prefer – shortcrust or ready-rolled puff pastry both work well.

Serves 4–6

- 900g potatoes
- 450g carrots
- 225g parsnips
- 450g cauliflower
- 225g swede
- 1 tablespoon oatmeal
- 1 vegetable stock cube
- a handful of freshly chopped parsley
- 3 sprigs of thyme
- 30g butter, softened
- 2 tablespoons Dijon mustard
- 1 tablespoon English mustard
- 3–4 spring onions, finely chopped
- 50g cheese, grated

- Preheat the oven to 190°C/Gas Mark 5.

- Cut half the potatoes, all the carrots, parsnips, cauliflower and swede into similar-sized pieces, put in a large saucepan and cover with water. Add the oatmeal and the vegetable stock cube and cook for about 10 minutes until the vegetables are just soft. Set aside to cool, then transfer to a pie dish. Scatter over the chopped parsley and the thyme leaves.

- Boil and mash the remaining potato. Add the butter, mustards and spring onions to the mashed potato then spread it over the top of the vegetables. Sprinkle with the cheese and bake until the top is golden brown and the filling is bubbling.

- Serve with an onion gravy or a squirt of tomato ketchup.

Pommes Anna

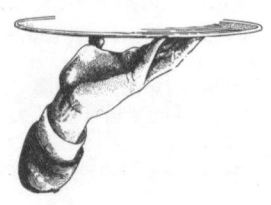

If there is one ingredient that can lay claim to being the backbone of global gastronomy, then the humble potato must have a pretty good case. Most vegetables would be happy just to be responsible for the chip, but oh no, the potato you can mash, roast, bake or simply boil to satisfying effect. Pommes Anna relies on the simple principle that the starch of the potato can act like a kind of gastro 'glue' creating a buttery, crispy potato cake that's like an edible plate for any juicy cut of meat.

As so often with gastronomic sorcery, the story of Pommes Anna begins in a great restaurant in Paris. From 1866, the Café Anglais was possibly the greatest restaurant of them all, thanks to a head chef called Adolphe Dugléré. Dugléré had been trained at the apron strings of one of the finest chefs the world has ever known, Marie-Antoine Carême, some of whose masterpieces are described elsewhere in this book.

This remarkable chef was immensely demanding, known to reject huge deliveries of vegetables if he considered them not of a high enough standard. He hated smoking and would not allow any cigars to be lit in the dining room until dinner was completely over, at which time the maître d' would move around the room lighting them for anyone that wished.

Dugléré created quite a few landmark dishes, including Sole à la Dugléré – poached fish on a tomato and onion concasse with a garnish of fresh parsley and a beurre blanc sauce – and, like many great chefs, he would name whole meals after important clients or visiting royalty. The men of influence who frequented Café Anglais did not dine alone; this was the time of the courtesans, high-class prostitutes who were part and parcel of life in the upper echelons of Paris society. They were known as *les grandes horizontales* (and I think the most rudimentary pidgin French-speaker can conjure up an image of what that means). One such was Anna Deslions, an aspiring actress who would often dine at the Café Anglais in the company of a man she hoped would fund her luxurious lifestyle while she waited for that big break. What made Dugléré create a special potato dish for her one night in 1868 is long forgotten and we know nothing of the man with whom she shared that first plate. Maybe the design was based around her untidy tumbling hair or the way her dress was constructed, who knows? Deslions, however, was part of a vibrant social circle and the popularity of a dish named after her was instant. Pommes Anna was the perfect accompaniment to roast meats, its circles of flat, buttery potatoes were pretty as a picture and it was soon on the menu of every grand restaurant in Paris. Like many of the French dishes in this book, Pommes Anna spread to America thanks to the indefatigable Julia Child and became popular thanks to the cult of the dinner party in the 1960s. Julia's recipe, like the original, uses a lot of butter and some purists still swear by this, but I think you get a good result with my slightly healthier approach.

In addition to his way with potatoes and with sole, Dugléré is remembered for creating perhaps the greatest dinner in French gastro-history. 'The Dinner of the Three Emperors' was commissioned by King William I of Prussia, a regular at the Café Anglais, with the specific instruction that no expense should be spared. Along with Tsar Alexander II of Russia, his son Alexander and Prince Otto von Bismarck, William sat down to a 16-course feast. The dining service and menu from this spectacular meal are still on display at Paris's oldest restaurant, Le Tour d'Argent.

Dugléré himself remains a mystery; his letters and belongings are on permanent display in the National Library in Paris, but they reveal very little about his culinary skill. His recipes were never catalogued, but we do know he was respected. Alexander Dumas consulted him frequently during his research for his *Great Dictionary of Cuisine* and when Dugléré passed away in 1884 the French press unanimously praised him, calling him the 'last great *cuisinier*'.

The French hold culinary genius in high esteem and these days you can even buy a special Pommes Anna pan to make the dish. Constructed from beaten copper by artisans in Normandy, it is a thing of great beauty. Can you imagine a British blacksmith lovingly crafting a Yorkshire pudding tray from the purest tin with his bare hands? One day, perhaps, but in the meantime get yourself a big slice of this perfect potato side dish and tuck in.

Pommes Anna

Crispy, savoury and delicious, Pommes Anna is one of my favourite potato dishes and goes well with meat or fish. Take your time when you layer the potatoes as you don't want it too thick or you won't get the crunch that makes this so special.

Serves 4–6

- 75g unsalted butter
- 750g potatoes
- salt and freshly ground black pepper

- Preheat the oven to 190°C/Gas Mark 5. Liberally butter a 23cm shallow pie dish. It is important you grease it well or the potatoes will stick.

- Peel the potatoes. Rinse under cold water and pat dry with kitchen paper. Cut the potatoes into slices about 3mm thick using a sharp knife or a mandolin slicer.

- Melt half the remaining butter in a saucepan and set aside.

- Line the pie dish with the potato slices, overlapping them slightly and in circles from the centre. Season with salt and pepper, then drizzle with some of the melted butter. Repeat and drizzle over more butter. Keep going until all the potatoes and butter have been used, pressing each layer down firmly as you go.

- Bake the potatoes for 30 minutes uncovered then remove, place a plate on top of the dish and turn the potatoes on to the plate.

- Then carefully slide the potatoes back into the dish so that the underside is now exposed. Cook for a further 20 minutes. Remove from the oven and leave the dish to cool for 5 minutes.

- Run a knife around the edge of the dish. Cover with a plate and turn out once more to serve. I cut it at the table but you can slice it into wedges if you prefer. I like to serve this with an oily fish such as sardines or mackerel. Just fillet the fish and lay it on top of the potatoes for the last 10 minutes of cooking with a little oil drizzled on top to keep it crispy. It is just as good with slices of roast beef or lamb though.

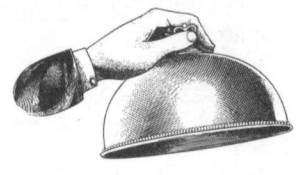

Pizza Margherita

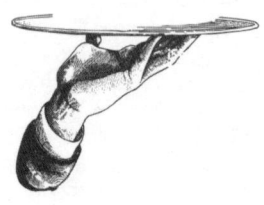

When you describe an oven-baked flat disc of bread topped with tomato sauce, cheese and various other ingredients, it is difficult to imagine how it has become the international staple fast food we all know and love. As with other great dishes in the culinary world, its simplicity and versatility hold the key.

We probably owe the modern-day pizza to the ancient Greeks, who were fond of flatbreads covered in oil, and to the Romans, who added a generous layer of cheese and honey with bay leaves. However, the real culinary magic started in the city of Naples. When exactly it began is anybody's guess, but it was certainly in full flow by around 1820 when, as the rumours go, King Ferdinand IV used to disguise himself as a peasant and walk the streets of Naples, devouring slices from every pizzeria he could find. (He had to do this because the royal court had banned the pizza, deeming it unsuitable for consumption by the monarchy – the fools!)

A basic Neapolitan pizza is tomatoes and mozzarella cheese on crispy dough. A recipe this simple requires some special ingredients and the real secret to the success of the pizza is down to just one – the San Marzano tomato. It grows on the plains of Mount Vesuvius, just outside the city, and feeds on the rare mix of nutrients that only an earth-shattering cataclysmic volcano can supply. The first San Marzano seedlings appeared in around 1770, apparently a gift from the King of Peru. Prior to that people had been eating the tasty but slightly seedy Romana variety, but soon the sweet, soft flesh and seedless texture of the San Marzano became the essential base of all Italian tomato-based cooking – which, let's face it, is about 90 per cent of the cuisine.

So towards the end of the nineteenth century we already have the Neapolitan pizza we recognize, being made with the ingredients it is made with today. It was quickly becoming the national dish for both rich and poor, so it was only fitting that in 1889, when a royal visit to Naples was scheduled, the palace should commission a renowned Neapolitan pizzaiolo, Raffaele Esposito, to create a pizza in honour of Queen Margherita. Esposito prepared three types for Their Majesties to try: one with pork fat, cheese and basil; one with garlic, oil and tomatoes; and another with mozzarella, basil and tomatoes, designed in the colours of the Italian flag. It was this last version that the Queen fell in love with. Pizza Margherita was born.

Word quickly spread and soon the Margherita was the benchmark by which all other pizzas were measured. Pizzas were now being devoured across Naples and beyond for breakfast, lunch and dinner. Not only that, but Italians were spreading their wings and heading to the developing Americas. They took with them the cooking techniques of their forefathers and soon realized they could turn these skills into profit.

New York and Chicago were the launch pads for a nationwide assault and the two cities produced pizza of great variety and distinctiveness. By the end of the nineteenth century, Chicago street pedlars were selling pizzas by the slice from metal containers, while in New York America's first pizzeria, Lombardi's, opened in 1905. Many put New York's success with pizza down to the high mineral content of its water supply. The difference is so marked that one restaurant in California found that the only way to get the authentic New York taste was to import water all the way from Manhattan to Beverly Hills. But that perhaps says more about the deepness of the pockets of the Beverly Hills clientele….

Pizza was well established in the United States by the time of the Second World War, but it was largely eaten by Italian immigrants and their families. It was servicemen returning from Italy in the 1940s, having discovered the joys of the local cuisine, who really spread the word: veterans ranging from the lowliest private to Dwight D Eisenhower came home clamouring for pizza. And, at about the same time Ric Riccardo and Ike Sewell of Chicago pioneered the 'deep pan' pizza, with a thicker and chewier base than the traditional crispy Neapolitan equivalent.

What is more pertinent perhaps is that in 2009 the European Union, upon Italian request, granted a Traditional Speciality Guaranteed label to Neapolitan pizzas and in particular to the Margherita. The Italians had seen the spread of pizza across the world, with many different toppings and styles, and it seemed that people might forget where it all began. Now the law states that an authentic Neapolitan Margherita pizza must use San Marzano tomatoes and fresh mozzarella, and it must be cooked on the premises, with no frozen produce. If only all countries were so forward-thinking.

 # Pizza Margherita

Once you have made your first pizza you will never look back. You need to be firm with the dough, making sure you sprinkle some polenta or semolina on the pizza shovel and pizza stone to stop the pizza sticking.

Serves 1–2

For the dough
- 400g strong white flour or '00' flour
- ½ tablespoon salt
- 1 sachet of dried yeast
- ½ tablespoon sugar
- 300ml tepid water
- 100g semolina, for dusting

For the topping
- 450g can San Marzano or plum tomatoes, pushed through a sieve to remove any last seeds
- 1 teaspoon salt
- Parmesan cheese
- 40g fresh mozzarella
- a handful of basil leaves
- olive oil
- freshly ground black pepper

- Pile the flour and the salt on to a board and make a well in the centre. In a bowl mix together the yeast, sugar and water until combined then leave the mixture to froth a little. Pour this into the well in the flour. Combine it slowly, drawing the flour into the water bit by bit. You will feel and see the dough forming. It will go through a wet stage but keeping combining it and it will begin to bind and become less sticky. Bring it into a ball.

- Now you need to knead your dough. I roll away from my body with the heel of my hand then lift the dough and flip it hard on to its back and bring the sides over. Some stretch with one hand whilst pulling with the other. It doesn't matter but the process needs to break the gluten and allow the dough to elasticize. It takes about 15 minutes and can be quite sweaty! Put the dough in an oiled bowl, cover with clingfilm and set aside for about 30 minutes. Put a pizza stone or upturned baking tray in the oven and turn it up as high as it will go. Most domestic ovens are not hot enough but a pizza stone will help get that base crispy.

- Pour the tomatoes into a saucepan with the salt and cook gently for 1 hour. Do not let them burn and add a little water if they begin to dry out. You only need a little for your pizza.

- Your dough should be enough to make four small pizzas. I prefer to prepare and cook each one individually. Cut the dough into four pieces, take one and roll it out very flat on a semolina-dusted surface. Transfer to your pizza shovel or a baking tray and make some finger indentations for a final stretch. Grate a little Parmesan cheese over it, then top with tomato sauce in a circular fashion. Add strips of mozzarella, then scatter over the basil leaves, drizzle with olive oil and season with pepper.

- Carry the pizza to the oven and transfer to the pizza stone or upturned baking tray. Bake for 5 minutes, then turn the pizza to ensure it is cooking evenly. Cook until the base has just turned dark at the edge and the topping is nicely cooked. Serve in slices on a board and enjoy with a cold glass of Fiano.

- Repeat for the remaining three balls of dough. If freezing, brush with olive oil and place in an airtight container or bag, ensuring that you remove as much air as possible. They should keep for 6 weeks. Make sure to defrost each one completely before using.

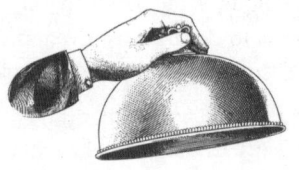

Tortellini

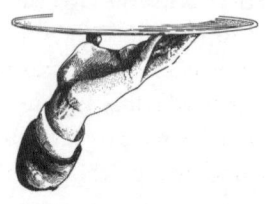

What is it about pasta that people love so much? It is probably the simplest thing in the world to prepare. It requires eggs and flour, nothing more. Once made it can be rolled into myriad shapes and designs, each as unique as the hands that make them. Maybe this is what appeals to the Italians. Even after Garibaldi had created a unified country (see page 246), the versatility of pasta meant that people could maintain regional distinctions and you could tell where you were by the pasta you ate.

The first recorded pasta was a simple flat lasagne sheet or *lagana*, documented as early as the fifth century, but by the 1400s thin strips or tagliatelle began to appear, followed by more intricate hand-rolled sorts such as macaroni. Tortellini was first recorded around that time, though they are probably much older. The creators were almost certainly Italian housewives who passed recipes on orally, as very few possessed strong writing skills. The filling was most commonly mortadella, a spicy cured pork particular to the area around Modena and Bologna. Bolognese cuisine included a lot of slow-cooked meaty ragús, which meant that filling thin sheets of pliable pasta with any cold leftovers made perfect sense to a frugal cook. The shape of tortellini is said to reproduce the turtle motif that is a feature of many seventeenth-century buildings in Modena.

However, Italians have a lust for life and a good story. Tortellini is traditionally made by hand by lines of people, rolling, filling, folding and pinching the dough for long hours. They swap tales with one another and this is the tale of Tortellini.

One night towards the end of the fifteenth century the notorious noblewoman Lucrezia Borgia was travelling from Modena to Bologna. Her notoriety was down to rumours of illicit, even incestuous, relationships with many partners, and of wild parties that sometimes ended in murder. Very little is actually recorded of Lucrezia, but there is no doubt about her allure for men. She had a pale complexion and is often depicted with vibrant red hair. On this particular night she had reached the small commune of Castelfranco Emilia and needed a place to rest. The local innkeeper was bewitched; so much so that when she retired to her room to bathe he followed her to spy on her. Restricted by the keyhole and the poor candlelight in the bedroom the peeping tom was unable to discern much. However, as Lucrezia stepped into her bath, he was given the merest of glimpse of her milky white stomach and the shadow of her navel.

Now, the fifteenth-century commune-dwelling Italian male was just as red-blooded as his modern counterpart, but given far less opportunity to express himself. So in his aroused state the innkeeper did what any man would do: he fled to the kitchen to produce a pasta so fine as to capture the beauty of Lucrezia Borgia's navel.

What happened next no one knows. Did he reveal his creation to his unknowing muse? Did she dine on it? We will never be sure, but it is a great story nonetheless.

Another version – told in Alessandro Tassoni's poem *'La Secchia Rapita'* or 'The Stolen Bucket', written around 1600 – says that the navel belonged to the goddess Venus, but tells a similar story of an infatuated innkeeper.

The reality is probably more mundane. But don't forget that Modena is also the home of Italy's great masculine icon, the Ferrari. There is no way that boring old practicality in either pasta-making or car manufacture is going to be celebrated in this town.

Celebration is a big part of Italian cooking. There are feast days for almost every ingredient, from mushroom events to chocolate and walnuts. Tortellini is no exception and it is the duty of The Learned Order of Tortellini to uphold its standard and ensure that future generations of Bologna's Tortellini are filled with the right stuff. Tradition states that light meats only should be used, mainly cured pork but also crab and sometimes chicken. The pasta is often served with the broth it has been cooked in, or in a buttery sage sauce. Tortellini should not be too large, but must be big enough to contain in one mouthful the flavours of Bologna.

For much of its history, Tortellini was hand-prepared, so it was mainly confined to the tables of the affluent who had plenty of time or servants to do the preparing. Twentieth-century mechanization meant that vast quantities could be produced and sold around the world, allowing Italian emigrants and other Europeans and Americans to enjoy the belly-button-shaped pasta gems.

Tortellini is wonderful to make yourself and even better to share with someone special, but when you have a go it is worth bearing in mind the old Italian proverb *'Il primo tortellini non riesce mai perfetto'*. This translates as 'the first Tortellini is never perfect'. So don't be discouraged and keep trying – you will get it.

 # Tortellini

This recipe is from the top Italian chef Francesco Mazzei, who is famed for championing dishes from the southern regions of his home country.

Serves 4

- 250g Italian '00' flour
- 3 eggs, plus 1 egg yolk
- 60g butter
- 1 shallot, chopped
- 150g burrata cheese
- 80g ricotta cheese
- 1g nutmeg
- 20g freshly chopped chives
- salt and freshly ground black pepper
- 30g sage leaves
- 40g hazelnuts
- 50g Grana Padano cheese
- 30g black truffle (optional)

- To make the pasta dough, put the flour in a bowl or on to a work surface. Make a well in the centre and crack the eggs into it. With a fork, carefully pull the flour from the edges into the centre, gradually mixing the flour and egg until smooth. Knead the mixture into a ball until the dough is firm but not sticky and then leave to rest under a bowl for about an hour.

- In a saucepan, sweat the shallot in half the butter until golden brown. Meanwhile, chop the burrata into small pieces and mix well with the ricotta, nutmeg, chives, salt and pepper. Add the cooked shallots.

- Divide the fresh pasta into four and keep three portions under a bowl while you roll and stuff one quarter. This prevents the pasta from drying out. Roll out the pasta into a long, wide strip about 1mm in thickness and cut into 6–7cm squares.

- Place a teaspoon of the filling in the centre of each square, brush some egg yolk around the edges and then close each parcel to form a rectangular shape, ensuring that no air is left inside and the sides are firmly closed. Repeat with the remaining dough. Cook the Tortellini in plenty of salted boiling water for approximately 5–6 minutes, then drain.

- Heat the remaining butter in a frying pan until it begins to foam slightly then add the sage leaves and coat them in the butter. Cook the sage until it is crispy and the butter has a slight brown colour and a nutty flavour. Do not let it burn.

- Serve the Tortellini on four plates and spoon over the butter and sage. Sprinkle with the hazelnuts (if they are large chop them slightly) and grate over the Grana Padano and the truffle if using.

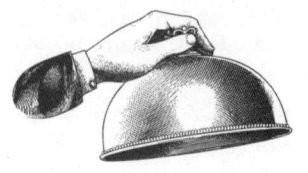

Pasta alla Norma

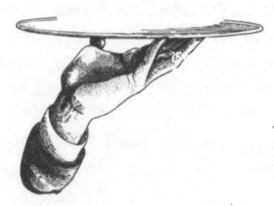

Sometimes the mere idea of a place conjures up exciting smells and appetizing experiences. Sicily is one example. It has an intense pride and gives its people a total sense of place, not to mention a food culture that is unique to the island. The dishes they produce can be both rustic and refined, but they share the same spirit – a boldness of flavour and bags of heart. Part of this comes from its being an island: once you cross the Messina Bridge you know you won't have to venture too far to be able to order one of the world's great pasta dishes.

Pasta alla Norma was not created by a big-name restaurant chef, but in the homes of everyday Sicilian people. It isn't complex; it features very few ingredients, but it must always, always, have aubergine and the very best ricotta cheese you can find. It is the combination of fleshy aubergine and the creamy, cheesy taste that makes this dish so good. It radiates the Mediterranean sun back at you from the plate; so much of that life-giving energy is needed to make the vibrant purple fruit that it is impossible not to taste it.

Sicilians don't just express themselves in their cooking, though: they also have their writings and their music, and it's these last two things combined that created the legend of Pasta alla Norma.

Vincenzo Bellini was born into a musical family in the town of Catania on the eastern tip of Sicily in 1801. He was composing music by the age of six; in 1831, having left Sicily to study in Naples and later Milan, he produced his masterwork, *Norma*. It's a powerful story of illicit love, infanticide, heartbreak, betrayal and eventually a double execution. The tragic heroine is thrown this way and that through every emotion as she battles to reconcile her abandonment with her love for her children. Norma is considered one of the greatest operatic figures, as well as one of the most difficult soprano roles in the repertoire, and her name signifies great passion and power.

Catania's prodigal son died young in 1835, but the good people of his home town remained very proud of him. Local impresarios and writers would congregate in the town hoping that some of the Bellini magic would rub off on them. One such man was Nino Martoglio, born in the nearby village of Belpasso, who pitched up in Catania in about 1890. He began writing poetry and produced pieces of theatre with his own company, all in Sicily's own language. He was instrumental in showing that the island tongue could be a literary force and he loved to hold court in the evenings, extolling its virtues. He was also well versed in the local cuisine and would devour it with passion. It was on one such evening of excited theatrics that he declared this simple dish of spaghetti with tomato and aubergine sauce topped with local salted ricotta the best thing he had ever eaten. He christened it 'alla Norma' in honour of the town's greatest creation and galvanized the people of Catania into claiming the dish as their local favourite: it served as a reminder on every menu in town that one of their own had left his mark on the world of opera.

The dish's fame was such that it eventually took flight and left the island. A population boom in southern Italy following the country's unification in 1861 meant that Italians had been leaving in large numbers, a trend that continued as two world wars ravaged Europe in the first half of the twentieth century. Many relocated themselves to the relative safety of the American urban areas; they lived in communities known as Little Italy and brought with them old ways of living and cooking, including recipes and flavours that were new to the people of America. Thus Pasta alla Norma found a whole new legion of fans.

These days we tend to think of Sicily as the home of the Mafia. This violent organization bears little resemblance to the first Mafiosi who came together to help Garibaldi liberate their beloved volcanic home. Through movies and television programmes we have romanticized the gangster lifestyle, but we have also learnt to appreciate the strength of the regional pride Sicilians have in the old ways – which always involve a huge appetite for rustic Italian dishes cooked in the way their mothers made them. Pasta alla Norma is one such dish. So when you make it – and you will – it will become clear to you why its ingredients haven't changed in well over a hundred years.

 # Pasta alla Norma

It may seem obvious but Italian cooking is all about the ingredients so obsess about their quality and try to get the best you can. Ricotta salata isn't the easiest thing to find but online retailers will deliver and if you have a good deli in your area they should be able to get it for you.

Serves 4

- 2 banana shallots, sliced into rings
- extra virgin olive oil
- 1 aubergine, cut into 2–3cm cubes
- large pinch of sea salt
- freshly ground black pepper
- 2 garlic cloves, crushed
- 1 teaspoon hot chilli flakes
- 450g San Marzano tomatoes (use any if you can't get these but it's better if you can)
- 400g penne rigate
- 50g ricotta salata (this is the salted drier version – make sure you get the right one)
- a handful of fresh basil leaves
- 50g Parmesan cheese, finely grated

- Preheat the oven to 180°C/Gas Mark 4. Fry the shallot rings in about 1cm of olive oil until crispy then drain on kitchen paper.

- Put the aubergine on a baking tray, coat in olive oil, season with salt and pepper then roast in the oven for about 20 minutes until it has softened.

- Heat a large frying pan over a medium heat, add a couple of tablespoons of olive oil and gently fry the garlic for a minute or two. Add the chilli. Crush the tomatoes – if you are feeling rustic then do this by hand, it's fun. Otherwise use a wooden spoon and squish them to a pulp. Add them to the garlic. Cook gently for about 10 minutes. Add the aubergine.

- Once the tomatoes are cooking, fill a saucepan with water and bring to the boil. Add a good amount of salt. Only add the pasta once the water is on a rolling boil and cook according to the packet instructions. The penne should be a little firm to the bite. Once it is ready, drain, reserving the water, and add the pasta to the tomato and aubergine. It needs to be tossed well and it will finish cooking in the sauce. If the sauce is at all dry then add a little of the pasta water.

- Crumble in the ricotta salata and allow it to warm slightly. It is a firm cheese so it won't melt. Scatter over the basil and serve topped with the shallot rings and the Parmesan to taste.

Pavlova

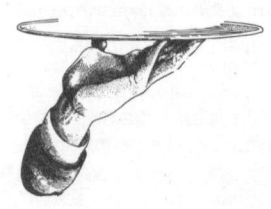

The great chef and former owner of Le Gavroche restaurant in London, Albert Roux, once told me a simple truth: 'No one needs a dessert. If the dinner has been good then everyone will be full, so a dessert has to be something special, an extra special treat.' Of course he is absolutely right. In terms of nutritional necessity, piles of sugary meringue covered in cream and an abundance of fresh fruit are wholly unnecessary, but boy, are they special. The Pavlova's dramatic entrance, topped with colourful berries, is beaten only by the shattering first slice of meringue just held together with unctuous creaminess. As slice after slice is devoured the last crumbs seem to cluster on the plate like the remains of snowmen in the park, just perfect for nibbling with port. It's no wonder the dish's place in culinary history is assured.

The origin of meringue is disputed, with one legend pointing toward a Swiss chef called Gasparini working in the small mountain town of Meiringen. This is dated at 1720, but in Britain there are recipes going back to the 1600s for beaten egg dishes called snow. The first written recipe using the word meringue seems to date from 1692, when it appears in a book by François Massialot called *Nouveau cuisinier royal et bourgeois*, translated into English in 1702.

So French chefs had been serving cream with meringue for quite some time when in 1926 New Zealand and Australia were preparing to entertain an exciting visitor. Anna Matveyevna Pavlovna Pavlova was the greatest ballerina of her time and some will argue that there has been none better since. Perhaps the greatest of her roles was The Dying Swan, which had been created for her by the choreographer Michel Fokine back in 1905. It was the perfect framework in which to display her unorthodox style of movement, which had eventually won people's hearts with its freedom and vulnerability.

It seems an obvious thing for a creative chef to have invented a dish in honour of Pavlova's visit, but the question that remains unsatisfactorily answered, and continues to divides New Zealanders and Australians, is, 'Which chef?'

New Zealanders assert that it was an unknown hotel chef in Wellington, while Australians attribute it to Herbert Sachse at the Hotel Esplanade in Perth. The first claim dates the recipe to 1926, in line with Pavlova's arrival, and the latter to a recipe in the Esplanade records for 1935. The discrepancy in the timing is put down to misfiling by Sachse. In between these two dates there are various documents across the region mentioning the dish, with versions popping up in magazines such as *Australian Woman's Weekly* and more obscure titles like the *Rangiora Mothers' Union Cookery Book*. What is certain is that 'meringue with fruit' recipes existed in many forms in both countries as early as 1926 and Pavlova is known to have danced in both nations, too. Sachse even admitted that he was inspired by a women's magazine recipe he had found, but claimed that the eventual, and now familiar, dessert was all his creation.

The argument has continued to rage and the absurdity of the culinary world's obsession with ownership has led to both Australia and New Zealand naming the 'Pav' as their national dish.

Whatever the truth is, the dessert captures Pavlova's spirit and profession perfectly. Its resemblance to a billowing tutu at the base with a colourful, vibrant fruit assembly on top helps to capture the dizzying brilliance of her dancing. Its own lifespan also seems to mirror that of Pavlova's famous feathered routine: the beauty fades quickly after creation and, unless it is consumed, the fruit and cream soon fall into the meringue and render it soggy and inedible – a dying dessert, if you will.

The dish's widespread popularity owes much to the dancer's cut-short career. Anna Pavlova died of pneumonia while touring Holland in 1931, aged only 49. In accordance with ballet tradition, on the day she was next to have performed, the show went on as scheduled, with a single spotlight circling an empty stage where she would have been.

Pavlova has allowed a global audience to remember one of the first international superstars, but it is also a blank canvas on which each territory can put its own stamp. The strawberry-obsessed English are just as keen to decorate it as the more tropical-loving French, who use passion fruit and mangoes. One of the great dinner-party celebration desserts lives on for a new generation to amend and evolve. So as you lay your meringue bases in the oven to cook, close your eyes and imagine those last fluttering movements of The Dying Swan and the greatest ballerina who ever lived.

 # Pavlova

Think spectacular here. This is a dessert meant to amaze and delight people – remember you are capturing the spirit of a woman who was able to do 37 consecutive spins on the back of an elephant. Now that is someone with a sense of theatre. I like to serve it whole at the table and just hand out spoons but you can dish it up if you like.

Serves 8

- 3 large fresh egg whites
  200g caster sugar
- 330ml whipping or double cream, whipped
- 300g soft fruits of your choice (strawberries and raspberries work well but bananas also do a good job)
- 1 tablespoon icing sugar

- Preheat the oven to 150°C/Gas Mark 2. Put the egg whites in a clean bowl (it has to be very clean) and whisk until they form firm, soft peaks. Don't be tempted to continue whisking as you will go too far and they will become looser again. Add the sugar gradually in small amounts and whisk after each addition until all the sugar is incorporated.

- Spoon half the mixture on to a baking tray covered with baking parchment or a silicone mat (non-stick is the key here) until it's about 24cm in diameter. Spoon out the rest in spoonfuls around the circle of egg white, then, using a fork or skewer, flick the meringue into peaks.

- Put in the oven and turn reduce the temperature to 130°C/Gas Mark 1 and cook for about an hour. After an hour turn the oven off and leave the Pavlova to cool completely. Do not remove it from the oven or it will become soggy when exposed to the air.

- Remove the Pavlova carefully from the baking parchment, spoon over the cream and top with the fruit. Dust with icing sugar and serve whole to the table and slice as desired.

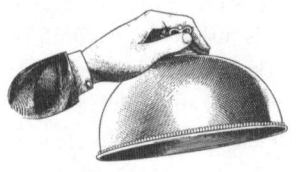

Apple Charlotte

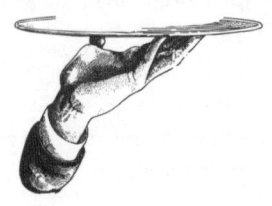

Mankind has a complicated relationship with the apple. From Adam's first innocent bite into the forbidden fruit it has woven its way into our everyday life and into a number of culinary masterpieces. An Apple Charlotte, with its brown crusty edges and warm, soft, sweet insides, is just about as comforting and filling as a dessert can be. The slight sharpness of the apple makes a perfect ending for a meal and prevents an overload of sugary depression. Best of all, it is really simple to make.

For many centuries apples have grown well in Britain and other countries, ranging from Turkey all the way to Argentina. Like much of the produce that is abundant in Britain today they are not indigenous, but were introduced by the Romans: long-serving army veterans were given settlements on which to grow fruit as part of their inducement to stay in Britain, and other less attractive outposts of the empire, after their term of service expired. Apple-growing lapsed a bit after the Romans left, but when, in 1066, William the Conqueror and his army from Normandy invaded, they restored the tradition throughout Britain. It survived almost three centuries, until the plague of 1349 wiped out half the population and left orchards uncared for.

It was in 1533, at the time of Henry VIII, that apples were reintroduced. Henry was a passionate foodie, as anyone who has looked at one of his portraits by Hans Holbein will be able to see. At his home in Hampton Court he gave his gardener, Richard Harris, the task of creating an orchard of many fruits, but in particular apples. Harris took lots of French varieties, such as custard and pearmain, and successfully planted and grew them. He distributed them to other farmers and was instrumental in the development of orchards across Kent, Herefordshire, Gloucestershire and Worcestershire – areas which to this day are associated with long lines of apple-bearing trees.

The other important ingredient of Apple Charlotte, bread, has been eaten across the world for thousands of years. As ways of using it up when it was past its best, puddings of bread soaked in milk, possibly mixed with fruit, and then baked were very much part of British cuisine by the mid-eighteenth century. At the same time, big country houses had started employing French-trained chefs and royal banquets abounded with apple desserts based on classic French recipes. It didn't take long for an unknown chef to turn the everyday pudding he was cooking into something more exciting.

The earliest known recipe was published in 1796 and named in honour of George III's Queen Charlotte. The royal couple lived mainly at Kew, in what is now the World Heritage Site of Kew Gardens. Charlotte became a keen gardener and from her horticultural base was able to champion the apple, eventually becoming the patron of the apple-growers of Britain. Her namesake pudding was soon copied by other chefs in other country houses. Different fruits were sometimes substituted for the apple – anything soft enough to cook down could be used – but the name Charlotte remained.

Then, early in the nineteenth century, the great French chef Marie-Antoine Carême came across the dish while he was working in England. He took the principle of a bread-bound pudding and, instead of serving it hot, made a cold custard filling and let it set. He replaced the bread lining with a more refined sponge finger biscuit and topped the whole thing with cherries. Carême stayed in England only a short time before moving to Russia to work, even more briefly, for Tsar Alexander I. It is possible that he named his version of the pudding Charlotte Russe in honour of his new employers – the Tsar's sister-in-law was called Charlotte. Or it may simply be a reflection of France's fascination with all things Russian at the time. There is even a version of the story that says Carême called his version *Charlotte à la Parisienne*, but changed it when it was served at a banquet in honour of the Tsar.

Despite being a very different dessert, Carême's creation has somehow maintained its Charlotte association to this day. Charlotte Russe made its way to other countries as the Russian aristocracy fled the revolutions of the early twentieth century; it was soon popular in many homes in America. Today, both it and Apple Charlotte grace dinner tables across the globe. On a cold autumnal Sunday nothing beats the crunchy buttered bread and soft sweet apple treat that is Apple Charlotte. Its ability to warm the heart should not be underestimated and it should be celebrated for going with not only piping hot custard but also double cream and, more importantly, both at the same time.

Apple Charlotte

A brilliant and simple dessert that is perfect on a blustery autumn weekend or if you live in Britain, a cold, wet Sunday in July! The Bramley is the perfect apple for this dish as it breaks down so well, but if you use it on its own the filling will be too mushy so do mix it with something firmer such as the Cox.

Serves 4–6

- 1.2kg apples (half Bramley and half Cox if possible)
- 2–3 tablespoons caster sugar (depending how sweet you like your puddings)
- 150g butter
- 6 slices of white bread, about 5mm thick with crusts removed
- 1 large egg yolk
- 1 teaspoon ground cinnamon

- Preheat the oven to 200°C/Gas Mark 6. Peel, core and thinly slice the apples, rinse them in cold water and put them in a saucepan with the sugar and half of the butter. Cook them over a low heat until they are soft enough to beat into a purée. Beat them and set aside to cool.

- Meanwhile, gently melt the remaining butter and cut each slice of bread into rectangles. Brush each piece of bread with melted butter on both sides, being careful not to leave any unbuttered patches. Line a 600ml pudding basin with approximately three-quarters of the bread (or as much as you need). Don't leave any gaps between the pieces – overlap them and press firmly.

- When the apple purée has cooled, beat in the egg yolk and ground cinnamon and fill the lined basin with the mixture. Finally seal the top with overlapping slices of the remaining bread. Place a suitably-sized ovenproof plate on top of the pudding and weight it down with a 900g scale weight. Set aside for 30 minutes.

- Bake the pudding (with the weight still on it) for 35 minutes. Then, with an oven cloth, remove the plate and weight and bake the pudding for another 10 minutes to brown the top.

- Remove from the oven and leave the pudding to settle in the basin for a minute before carefully inverting it on to a warmed plate to serve.

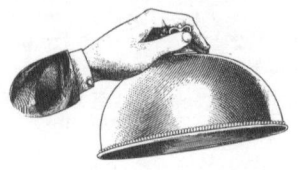

Bananas Foster

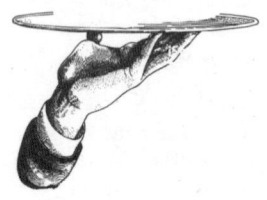

The world is full of weird and wonderful things to eat, and the humble banana started out as one of them. Imagine the excitement when, in the 1600s, European explorers returning from North America first laid a bright yellow bundle of finger-like fruit at the feet of their rulers. The principal banana port on mainland America was New Orleans, so it makes sense that our most exciting banana recipe should have its origins in that fascinating and turbulent city.

Bananas Foster is an all-American dessert – it is rich, it is bold and it is sweet. It's also a dish that can be prepared tableside, a piece of theatre. For those who see bananas as a lunchbox snack, now is the time to think again. This mixture of buttery caramel and softened fruit flamed with rum is the perfect antidote to the spiciness of a traditional Cajun meal.

The banana is a tough ingredient to be creative with. It is starchy and firm, so is difficult to incorporate into traditional French-style desserts: it is likely to come out heavy and less than ornate. Then again, a fully ripe banana is soft, mushy and tends to discolour, turning anything it touches to the same unappetizing brown. Bananas also lack the sharpness of a citrus fruit and are therefore not great with rich, eggy puddings. So when in 1951 the owner of Brennan's restaurant in New Orleans set his head chef, Paul Blangé, the challenge of creating a new banana pudding, it wasn't as straightforward as you'd think.

Owen Brennan had run a bar in Bourbon Street for some time, in an old absinthe house and pirate hang-out. He had renovated a 'secret room' where pirates and revolutionaries had once drunk and which now became a place for Hollywood stars and politicians to drink undisturbed. Then, in 1946, he opened a restaurant just across the street. It was a family place; Brennan employed his father, two of his sisters and his brother. The local diners loved their 'Blarney Stone' patter, but Brennan was committed to promoting his beloved New Orleans and wanted the area's unique culinary larder to be at the forefront of the menu – the restaurant served classic Cajun food: gumbos, stews, seafood, all of which people loved.

As a result of this civic pride Brennan became friends with other local champions, one of whom was Richard Foster, chairman of the New Orleans Crime Commission and owner of a local awning company. He and Brennan shared a desire to clean up the streets of New Orleans and help it develop as a tourist destination, so he was frequently in the restaurant to talk and to eat.

Now, back to the banana challenge. *Holiday* magazine had requested a recipe that summed up Brennan's but also represented the area. Paul Blangé, a Dutchman who had worked at Brennan's since it opened, knew that what was needed was an event. Bananas were big business in the region – it was only right to celebrate them. The most famous pudding at the time was a baked bread pudding, which usually came with a whisky sauce. This got Blangé thinking about the area's other great liquor, rum. Rum and bananas…rum flambés…bananas are great charred – you can feel the logic of a great idea developing.

And so the autumn 1951 edition of *Holiday* got its recipe and Brennan's restaurant got a dessert that would become an international favourite and has never left the menu in over 50 years. It made perfect sense for Brennan to name the dish after his friend and fellow conspirator, Richard Foster. Today it is cited as New Orleans' favourite dessert and as the interest in Cajun cooking worldwide has grown others have copied and used the dish for their own menus.

Brennan himself died in 1955, suffering a heart attack after an indulgent banquet. He would have been proud to see so many people across the world enjoying New Orleans cuisine. His restaurant moved around the corner in 1956, but remains as popular as ever. As for Foster, his awning company still exists, with several outlets across America.

Chef Paul Blangé passed away in 1977 and, in a twist in keeping with New Orleans' link with the supernatural, people believe that his spirit haunts the kitchens of Brennan's. He was buried with a knife, a fork and a copy of the restaurant menu and many a chef has reported hearing knocking at the kitchen door only to find the hallway empty. So when you're at home with your rum burning brightly, don't be alarmed if you hear a gentle tapping at the kitchen window. It's just Paul Blangé and he wants his bananas!

Bananas Foster

Brennan's restaurant flambés around 16,000kg of bananas every year and once you have a go you will see this dish's visual power. It really is best served in front of your guests – sit them down, even put on some jazz, but get all your ingredients ready first and go for it. There is nothing like seeing the smile on someone's face illuminated by the flash of rum as its flame leaps off the pan.

Serves 4

- 50g butter
- 200g brown sugar
- ½ teaspoon ground cinnamon
- 55ml banana liqueur
- 4 bananas, cut in half lengthwise, then halved
- 55ml dark rum
- 4 scoops of vanilla ice cream

- Combine the butter, sugar and cinnamon in a flambé pan or skillet. Put a saucepan over a low heat on an alcohol burner or on the hob, and cook, stirring, until the sugar dissolves. Stir in the banana liqueur, and then add the bananas. When the bananas soften and begin to brown, carefully add the rum. Continue to cook the sauce until the rum is hot, then tip the pan slightly to ignite the rum.

- Put a scoop of ice cream into four serving dishes. When the flames subside, lift the bananas out of the pan and place four pieces over each portion of ice cream. Generously spoon warm sauce over the top of the ice cream and serve immediately.

Baked Alaska

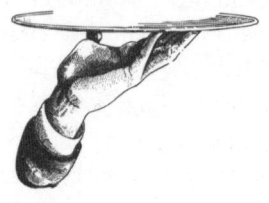

Cooking always involves a bit of chemistry, but in the case of Baked Alaska there is quite a lot going on and that's what makes it such a magical dish. How can any diner not have their socks blown off by the wonderful sensation of crispy hot meringue giving way to a ball of freezing cold ice cream beneath?

Whipping egg whites into meringue has been going on since the eighteenth century, but it was only around the turn of the nineteenth century that super-chefs like Marie-Antoine Carême began to use piping bags to embellish desserts and in particular to form meringues. Suddenly it became possible to squeeze pipes of swirling egg white as high as your imagination could go!

Around the same time the great culinary minds of the world were also examining the way in which heat affected different elements of a dish when applied to all of them at the same time. Benjamin Thompson, born in Massachusetts in 1753 but working in Britain, experimented with encasing solid ice and ice cream in beaten egg white and baking them in an oven; he discovered that the ice and cream held their shape while the egg solidified. Thompson left the world of gastronomy there and spent his later life developing insulation for fireplaces and thermal underwear, but other chefs took his findings and ran with them. Soon menus across Europe, America and Australia were full of omelette surprise or *omelette norvégienne* (records do not show why it was called a Norwegian omelette – possibly because Norway was thought of as a particularly cold place). There's even a story that the idea was passed on to a French chef by a Chinese delegation visiting Paris in 1866 – who knows?

It took a showman of Barnum-like proportions to give the dish its current persona and stamp it with a name that was to stick forever. This chef was Charles Ranhofer. Ranhofer became the chef at Delmonico's at New York in 1862, and steadily turned this already great restaurant into something very special indeed, giving his lavish banquets a bit of the magic that New York is still famous for. One particularly decadent affair saw him set a pond filled with swans inside the dining room so that his diners could feel they were by the banks of a lake.

So where does Alaska fit in to all this? Well, there were Russian settlers in Alaska, but they had never fully colonized it, believing it to be unprofitable. So when in 1867 the US Secretary of State William H Seward offered Russia a whopping $7.2 million for it, the negotiations were short. People referred to the purchase as Seward's folly, but he was later proved right with discoveries of gold, natural gas and oil.

Whichever way you look at it the deal was big news, so when, back in New York, Seward held a state banquet to honour the occasion it seemed only fitting for it to be held at Delmonico's. Ranhofer's moment of genius came in the choice of Omelette Surprise as dessert. What better dish could there have been? Its billowing peaks of meringue were reminiscent of the icy wasteland of America's newest territory. Ranhofer's version involved a hollowed-out génoise sponge cake with ice cream inside; the whole dish was placed in the freezer, then covered in piped meringue and baked in Delmonico's fiercely hot ovens. It was an absolute masterpiece and it went down like an Alaskan snowstorm.

The dish's fame spread across New York and soon the whole of America was aware of the newly named Baked Alaska. Restaurants loved its wow factor and when, in

1896, the recipe appeared in Fannie Farmer's *Boston Cooking-School Cookbook* its place in American kitchens was assured. By that time the dish was also on the menu of the Hôtel de Paris in Monte Carlo, where it became synonymous with the rich and famous and was considered the height of luxury.

Chefs can do more dramatic things with their tools these days and there is even an inverse baked Alaska recipe that uses a microwave oven to create a liquid hot centre in a frozen outer case. Scientist Nicholas Kurti proposed such a recipe to the members of the Royal Society in London in 1969.

Nowadays people have good ovens at home, and blowtorches too, so they can scorch their meringues with ease. If you ask me, oven baking is the only way to create that delicious moment of uncertainty that turns an ordinary meal into an unforgettable one, but if you have a blowtorch then feel free to use it. I suppose it's the difference between having and not having a safety net. Ranhofer would probably approve of the flamboyance, especially if you serve your Baked Alaska on a pond with a couple of swans!

 # Baked Alaska

This is probably one of the most exciting dishes to make at home. It has risk and danger but in the end if you pull it off you will feel like a million dollars, or 7.2 million dollars in fact. The ice cream must be very frozen if you are to be successful.

Serves 4

- 500ml good-quality vanilla ice cream
- 3 medium egg whites
- 90g caster sugar
- 90g icing sugar, sieved
- 1 large sponge flan case, cut in half widthways to about 5mm thick
- 4 tablespoons raspberry liqueur (I use Chambord)
- 8 tablespoons raspberry jam

- In advance take the ice cream from the freezer so it softens slightly and scoop out four good golf-ball-sized helpings. Put these on a tray back in the freezer. Preheat the oven to 240°C/Gas Mark 9.

- Whisk the egg whites in a very clean bowl adding the caster sugar a little at a time as you go. You want stiff white peaks. Now add the icing sugar and mix it slowly to start with then faster as you continue, otherwise you will vanish in a cloud of dust. Again you want stiff peaks but also a shiny texture.

- Cut the sponge into four rings with a 7.5cm cutter and put on a baking tray. Divide the liqueur evenly between them. Spread the jam over the sponge then sit a scoop of ice cream on top of each one.

- Transfer the meringue to a piping bag and pipe over the ice cream. Start by covering the top then spread down the sides with a palette knife. Then add a second layer more intricately any way you wish, but a swirl is quite pretty. Make sure the sponge and ice cream are completely covered. If you wish you can freeze the whole Alaskas at this point if you are making them in advance for a dinner party.

- Now put the Alaskas in the oven or if you like you can blowtorch them, but you won't get a crispy meringue, just a nice colour. Remove from the oven once the meringue has got a touch of colour and has gone only a little hard – probably about 5 minutes.

- Serve immediately.

Crêpes Suzette

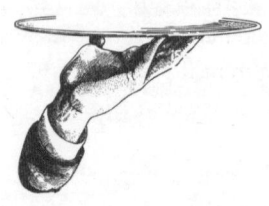

There are surely few things more exciting in a recipe than the word 'flambé'. It means a moment of drama, a controlled explosion of gases, a colourful flame. It guarantees a gasp of admiration. Combine this with that great piece of culinary acrobatics, the flip, and you have yourself a pretty solid piece of theatrical cooking. The glowing, seductive, buttery sauce poured over a childhood favourite, the pancake, makes Crêpes Suzette a winner every time, and whether or not you add a ball of ice cream is neither here nor there. You can't help but feel warm inside – literally, sometimes!

However, for something so universally admired, its story is full of dispute. I present to you the two conflicting claims to its beginnings.

The first comes in the form of an ambitious, 14- or 15-year-old waiter called Henri Charpentier. The year was 1895, the height of the Belle Époque or 'beautiful era', a time of great optimism in France. Framed by the newly finished Eiffel Tower, the Paris World Fair of 1889 had lit the touch paper for a generation. Science and the arts were seeing a period of expansion and innovation, and the rich and famous were able to travel in fancy motor cars and drink even better champagne. This was a good time to be running a restaurant if you could attract the right clientele and the Café de Paris in Monte Carlo attracted only the best.

One night the great and good came in the form of Edward, Prince of Wales, the future Edward VII of England. Somehow Henri Charpentier found himself tasked with serving dessert to the Prince and his friends, including the daughter of one of them, a frankly untraceable young lady called Suzette. The citrus-sauced pancake was always prepared at tableside in a chafing pan and this night of all nights the young Charpentier royally mucked it up. The crêpes went up in flames, but this apparent disaster seemed to give the dish the magic it needed. Henri still served it and later reported, 'The prince ate the pancake with a fork and then used a spoon to enjoy the remaining syrup.' It was Edward himself who asked that it be named Crêpes Suzette in honour of his young companion.

This all sounds very believable but we have only Charpentier's own account, which he published in his memoir, *Life à la Henri*, in 1934. By that time he had moved to the United States, built up quite a reputation for his cooking and opened a restaurant on Long Island whose guests included Presidents Theodore Roosevelt and Woodrow Wilson, no less.

There is no doubt that Charpentier was instrumental in making Crêpes Suzette as popular as it is today. He went on to serve it at many of the world's top restaurants, including the Café Royal and the Savoy in London and the Metropole in Moscow, as well as across America. He even worked for a short time under the great Auguste Escoffier, who was incidentally the first to record a recipe for the dish, in his *Guide Culinaire*. However, Charpentier's story is called into question by some highly regarded publications, including *Larousse Gastronomique*, which points out that he was far too junior to be given charge of serving the Prince anything, let alone making his dessert tableside.

The second explanation also comes from a debatable source. In 1897 an actress named Suzanne Reichenberg was starring at the famous Parisian theatre, La Comédie Française. She played a parlourmaid and part of the story involved her serving pancakes to some of the other characters. The food was prepared every day at a local restaurant,

Le Marivaux, under the supervision of its proprietor Monsieur Joseph, but to make the pancakes more visible to the audience the actress flambéed them live on stage. Joseph came up with the name Crêpes Suzette in her honour; he too later worked at the Savoy in London and reputedly served the pancakes there, under the watchful eye of Escoffier, adding an even more intriguing layer to our tale.

A third suggestion is that the dish was created by a chef named Jean Redoux for King Louis XIV in honour of Princess Suzette of Carignan, but only those with the strongest love of the unlikely give this theory any credence.

We'll never know for certain which story is true and in the end it doesn't much matter. But the idea that the great British playboy king was in some way responsible for one of the most exciting of puddings is deliciously appealing. Don't you think?

 # Crêpes Suzette

People call this dish retro but don't listen to them. It's just as exciting as it was back in the 1890s and is a great end to a dinner party. Warm the Grand Marnier before flaming and dip the lights to make sure you catch its blueish glow as you carry it to the table.

Serves 4

For the crêpes
- 110g plain flour
- pinch of salt
- 1 egg, plus 1 egg yolk
- 200ml milk mixed with 100ml water
- 1 tablespoon vegetable oil, plus extra for frying
- zest of 1 medium orange
- 1 tablespoon caster sugar

For the sauce
- 150ml orange juice (from 3–4 medium oranges)
- zest of 1 medium orange
- zest and juice of 1 small lemon
- 1 tablespoon caster sugar
- 50g unsalted butter
- 50ml Grand Marnier, for flaming

- Sift the four and salt into a bowl. Beat the egg and egg yolk together and make a well in the centre of the flour and pour in the eggs. Using a whisk slowly begin to combine the eggs and the flour, drawing the flour in from the edges. Add a little of the milk and water mixture to loosen the mixture. When the mixture becomes dry add a little more of the milk. Keep whisking constantly – you are trying to avoid any lumps. Add all the milk until the mixture is fully combined. You want a thin consistency. Now add the oil, orange zest and sugar then cover the bowl. Chill in the fridge for 30 minutes.

- Brush a flat frying pan with oil, add a ladleful of batter and slowly tip the pan so it covers the base. The batter should set if the pan is hot enough. Leave it for a minute or two. Loosen the edges with a spatula if you are worried but leave the pancake to cook a little or it will stick. Turn the pancake when it has a nice golden colour on the bottom and cook through. Remove from the pan on to a warm plate and cover with baking parchment. Repeat with the remaining batter.

- To make the sauce, combine the orange and lemon juice and zest with the sugar. Melt the butter in a saucepan and add the sauce slowly. Fold each pancake into quarters and put them into a warmed serving dish. Add the liqueur to the sauce and leave it to warm. You should be able to light it now either with a match or by carefully tipping your pan over the flame on the hob. When it is alight, dim your lights and pour over the pancakes then serve immediately.

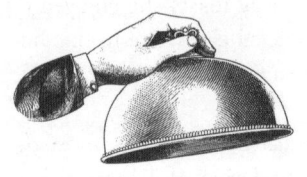

Peach Melba

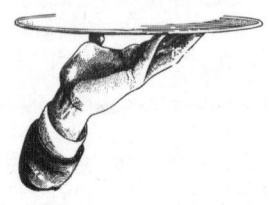

     ow you are a pretty special person to have a single dish named after you during your lifetime, let alone two. In fact the Australian operatic soprano Dame Nellie Melba has four dishes that bear her name. The story of the fabulously crispy toasts she enjoyed on her Savoy Hotel sickbed is chronicled elsewhere in this book. The remaining two, a sauce and a truffled chicken, I shall leave to other pens.

Peach Melba must be one of the most perfect desserts ever made, a sweet and colourful beauty that has adorned the menu of most of the greatest restaurants in the world. I doubt there is a person reading this who doesn't secretly want a little taste of the sweet, succulent peach and raspberry pud right now.

Such a perfect dish has a suitably grand beginning, thanks to probably the most complete chef the world has ever known, Auguste Escoffier. As is recorded elsewhere in this book Escoffier was an innovator in many ways. Not only was he a culinary genius, he was also a pretty savvy businessman and was highly successful at running hotel restaurants.

It was while working in Monte Carlo after the Franco-Prussian War of 1870–1 that Escoffier met César Ritz. Thus was born the now legendary partnership that brought Escoffier to London to work with Ritz first at the Savoy and later at Ritz's own hotels, the Carlton and the Ritz, where both would make their fortunes.

So in the early 1890s Escoffier was happily redefining the world's cooking habits at the most glamorous of venues, the Savoy Hotel. Nellie Melba was already a global star and a frequent visitor to both Covent Garden and the Savoy. At the end of 1892, she was playing to packed houses in Wagner's *Lohengrin*, a fairy-tale opera full of noise and magic in which one of the characters has been turned into a swan.

She was also being courted by Prince Philippe I, Duke of Orléans, and they entertained and were entertained often in the Savoy's grand restaurant. When Philippe decided to throw a lavish dinner in Nellie's honour, he obviously turned to the world's favourite chef to provide the food.

Never one to disappoint, Escoffier threw the works at it. To finish he wheeled out a swan sculpted entirely of ice on which were piled soft, succulent peaches on a bed of creamy, vanilla-heavy ice cream. On top was a web of woven spun sugar. It was a masterpiece, its elegance beaten only by its beauty. Melba herself always feared that ice cream would ruin her vocal cords, but Escoffier's cunning in combining it with meringue and fruit raised the temperature just enough for her to be able to enjoy it while still protecting her precious instrument.

At the time, Escoffier named the dish *Pêches au Cygne* or 'peach swan', but he recreated it a few years later to help celebrate the opening of the Carlton Hotel. This time he placed a more practical dish on the dessert menu: it came without a sculpted swan but with the addition of a redcurrant and raspberry purée. Escoffier called this Melba Sauce, and gave the dish a new name of Peach Melba. He quickly recognized the sauce's versatility – the 1907 English translation of his *Guide to Modern Cookery* says that 'the majority of English puddings may be accompanied by stewed fruit, Melba sauce or whipped cream' and he recommends it as an accompaniment to strawberries and pears as well as peaches. Today Melba Sauce can go with a whole variety of things from meringue to sponge cake. It is simple to create but shows off the very best of summer produce. Its colours are unmistakable, another Escoffier trait. He loved bright ingredients and used a wide palette on the plate.

Other chefs watched – and read – Escoffier closely and soon the dish was appearing on rival menus all over London and Europe. It quickly transported itself down under to Australia, too, and was served at many a dinner in Nellie's honour.

The name Melba is now so inextricably linked with the world of gastronomy that I would hazard a guess that more people are familiar with the food references than with the Aussie songstress's operatic career. There is one irony hidden among all this, though – Melba was not Nellie's real name; it was derived from her home town of Melbourne. But Peach Mitchell just doesn't have the same ring to it!

Peach Melba

Peaches come in a few varieties – the white are nice if you can get hold of them but better for making cocktails. I like the sweeter red peaches for this dish with their orange flesh giving a nice colour contrast.

Serves 4

- 4 ripe peaches
- 500g caster sugar
- 1 vanilla pod
- 300g raspberries
- 2 teaspoons icing sugar
- a squeeze of lemon juice
- vanilla ice cream

- Plunge the peaches into boiling water for 30 seconds then leave to cool. Remove the skins and set aside.

- Put 1 litre water into a large saucepan, add the sugar and bring to the boil. Split the vanilla pod and add to the water. Once bubbling nicely, allow it to simmer for 5 minutes, then add the peaches. Poach the peaches gently for 6–7 minutes until a knife pierces them without pressure. Remove from the water and leave to cool completely.

- Cut the peaches in half and remove the stones. Put the raspberries, icing sugar and lemon juice in a food processor and blitz until smooth. Strain through a sieve to remove the seeds.

- To serve, layer each bowl with ice cream, put two halves of peach on top then cover in the raspberry purée. If you are brave then garnish with spun sugar, or if less brave toasted flaked almonds are a nice addition. You can also add a few extra raspberries if you wish.

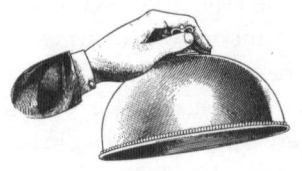

Tarte Tatin

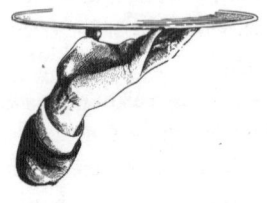

There are some recipes that will be around forever, some desserts that always have the power to bring a smile. If there are two words whose appearance on a menu means you have to plan your meal carefully, knowing that room must be kept at the end, those words are Tarte Tatin. It has that sticky sweet brownness that makes your mouth water; the crunch of the pastry that makes your stomach sing as you bite it; the smell of caramel that takes you right back to every fairground you ever went to. Perfection is never achievable in cooking but if you were to try to describe it, Tarte Tatin would be a pretty good way to start.

Its story is one of the best known in culinary circles and most people will know some or all of it. It concerns a pair of sisters, Stéphanie and Caroline Tatin, who, around 1880, were running a hotel in Lamotte-Beuvron, a small town in the region of Sologne in north-central France. At the end of the nineteenth century the food of the region reflected its terroir: it was full of gamey flavours, wild boar and foraged leaves, often paired with orchard fruits from newly planted woodlands. Hunters would come and stay at the Hôtel Tatin during the season to shoot at tiny birds with big guns and then eat heartily. Caroline, an even-tempered woman, ran front of house, while the more fiery Stéphanie was in charge of the kitchen.

Food scholars are divided as to the reason why Stéphanie cooked the traditional apple pie upside down; there are those who believe it was a complete error and those who feel it was a great rescue of a spoilt pie filling. Any cook will identify with that moment of panic when you realize that your carefully worked out timetable has fallen apart, so it is not hard to imagine Stéphanie realizing she was running late, turning her oven up full, throwing her apples in their usual butter and sugar and then forgetting all about them. What distracted her we will never know, but the smell of burning certainly got her attention. The apples were no good for the pie she had planned to make, but, thinking fast, she grabbed her pastry, rolled it out and placed it over the top in an attempt to salvage something. Sologne had a long history of upside-down puddings and the great Marie-Antoine Carême had described what he called *gâteaux renversés* topped with apples nearly a hundred years earlier. So it is wholly believable that Stéphanie's improvisation was supported by the conviction that something edible would emerge.

She may have anticipated that she would avoid disaster, but she couldn't have predicted the response to her new dish, served hot from the oven. Customers just loved it. It was the making of the hotel. But how does an apple pie from a remote hotel in a French woodland town become one of the most famous puddings in the world?

Well, as with so many of the recipes in this book, Stéphanie's upside-down tart attracted many imitators. But the story of how it made it to Paris is almost certainly not true. In the 1930s the great restaurant in the capital was Maxim's and its future owner, Louis Vaudable, later perpetrated a story that he had hunted in the area around Lamotte-Beuvron, discovered and been captivated by the tart, and stolen the recipe from the Tatins while working undercover as a gardener – or possibly having sent a spy disguised as a gardener. Sadly, this is probably artistic licence: Louis was only four when the sisters retired in 1906 and his father Octave didn't take over Maxim's until 1932. However, sometime during the 1930s the dish was placed on the menu and has never left it. Maxim's credited the dish to les demoiselles Tatin – the sisters themselves had always called it *tarte solognote*, after their home region – and so the name Tarte Tatin was born. Maxim's endorsement was enough to assure its place in gastronomic history (though in America yet again Julia Child did her bit) and it soon began to evolve: these days you are just as likely to get a savoury tatin with tomatoes and olives as you are a cherry one. The use of different pastry is also common. The original uses a simple shortcrust pastry, but some people argue passionately that puff pastry is better.

Myself I prefer puff and as for the choice of apple, well, those lucky Tatin ladies used Reinettes, but they are tricky to come by at my local greengrocer. I go for Cox or Granny Smith – you need texture and bite. Otherwise there is little change in all these years from that very first upside-down piece of heaven.

Tarte Tatin

Well here it is, probably the best known of all the dishes in this book. It is easy to burn the sugar so don't let it get too brown before adding the apples. You need that rich caramel to bring the whole dish together and any burnt sugar will add an unwanted bitterness to the finished tart.

Serves 6

- 6 medium Cox or Granny Smith apples
- 100g butter
- 100g golden caster sugar
- 375g packet all butter ready-rolled puff pastry

- Preheat the oven to 220°C/Gas Mark 7. Peel and core the apples. You can do this the day before and leave them in the fridge as the dry air in the fridge helps to crisp them up. They will go brown but it doesn't matter for this dish.

- Melt the butter in a 20cm tarte tatin tin or in an ovenproof skillet over a medium heat. Add the sugar and stir it slowly so that it dissolves into the butter. Watch it carefully and when it starts to turn brown put the apples in. Place them with the cored side up (remember you are making an upside-down tart) making sure they are covered in the caramel. Cook for about 10 minutes until they start to soften. Remove from the heat.

- Carefully unroll the pastry and prick it all over with a fork. Cut it to the size of the tin leaving a couple of centimetres extra around the edge, then lay it over the apples. Quickly turn the excess down the sides of the tin and put the tart in the centre of your oven. Bake for 25 minutes but check frequently in the last 5 to make sure the pastry doesn't burn. Remove from the oven and leave it to rest for a minute. Loosen the edges with a knife and place your serving plate over the tin, serving-side down, then flip the tin allowing the tart to come out. Be confident and it will work.

- Slice and serve warm with ice cream. It is best eaten quickly to prevent the pastry from softening.

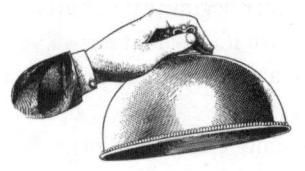

Battenberg Cake

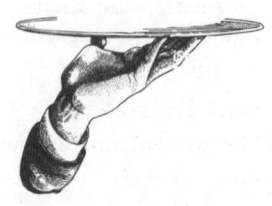

Young or old there can't be a person alive who doesn't smile at the sight of the yellow and pink squares of a Battenberg Cake – the sweet marzipan coating giving way to a light, delicate sponge with the merest tang of apricot jam. Its story begins two hundred or so years ago and in commercial form it's been on our supermarket shelves for the best part of a century. Its hypnotic chessboard effect is an early example of decorative cake-making and whether it's presented plainly on a white plate with a pot of tea or dressed with icing curls and tuile biscuits it still mesmerizes us today. In some ways it is uniquely British, too – it is rarely seen in other countries and it is fitting that it owes its existence to a royal wedding.

The Battenberg family was a watered-down branch of one of the grand duchies of old Germany, created to cope with an off-piste relationship in 1851. Prince Alexander of Hesse and by Rhine married beneath him, but to avoid social embarrassment the bride was allowed to call herself Countess of Battenberg. The title was upgraded to Princess in 1858, though there is not and has never been a principality of Battenberg.

The Battenbergs then spread themselves far and wide across Europe's royal families. Queen Victoria was a prolific matchmaker and in 1862 paired off her daughter Alice to one of Hesse's Grand Dukes. Twenty years later she saw another opportunity to firm up relations with Germany via Alice's daughter, Princess Victoria of Hesse. The Queen made it very clear that Louis of Battenberg, son of that first Countess and now serving in the British Navy, was to do the honourable thing and marry his first cousin once removed. The Princess's father strongly disapproved, but coincidentally he also married on the same day, to his commoner mistress – a marriage that he later tried to annul.

So in Damstadt, Germany, on 30 April 1884, a small royal contingent turned out for what in society terms was a quiet affair. But every wedding needs a cake and this wedding had *the* cake. Created by the royal party's own kitchen, it was resplendent. Its pink and yellow squares of sponge were an edible reflection of the Battenberg coat of arms; encased in sweet almond marzipan and served in small slices, each plateful was a colourful reminder of the royal couple's heritage. (There is another theory that the four squares represented Louis and his three brothers, but no reference to this has ever appeared anywhere official and there was no suggestion at the time that the princes were the design inspiration for the cake.)

Still based in Britain, Prince Louis rose to be First Sea Lord, but was asked to resign after the First World War broke out in 1914: the war led to a lot of anti-German feeling in England and very few sat down to enjoy a slice of a German-sounding cake as they listened to news from the Western Front. The Battenbergs even changed their name to appear more English; Louis finally relinquished his ties to the Duchy of Hesse in 1917, becoming instead the Marquess of Milford Haven and adopting the family name Mountbatten.

For some years following the war the cake remained unloved and uncelebrated. Then in 1938 J Lyons and Company decided to branch out from serving tea to making confectionery, and so launched our love affair with the Battenberg. The Lyons Corner Houses were hugely popular and were always buzzing with people eating cakes and enjoying pots of tea. It made business sense for Lyons to expand their cake-making to industrial levels so that they could sell them directly to shoppers elsewhere.

The Battenberg was in their launch range and was an instant crowd-pleaser. Its German heritage long forgotten, it was its glorious Technicolor appearance that made teatime special. For a while business was good, very good. Lyons' distinctive vans travelled the length and breadth of the country, stocking up shops with cakes and biscuits. However, in the 1960s the company fell into decline; bit by bit their business interests were sold off, with Kipling eventually taking on their cake production. The strict and varied control of food dyes in other countries has limited Battenberg's chances of global domination, but British children still peel off the marzipan wrapping and separate the squares wide-eyed, just as their ancestors did. No other cake delivers in quite the same way on your teatime trolley or, better still, atop a three-tiered cake stand.

Battenberg Cake

To make your own Battenberg is something of an endeavour, but it is a brilliant way to spend a rainy afternoon and for those who don't like using artificial food colourings there are beetroot-derived powders now available that you can use.

Serves 4–6

- 100g butter, softened
- 100g golden caster sugar
- 100g self-raising flour
- 50g ground almonds
- ½ teaspoon baking powder
- 2 medium eggs
- 1 teaspoon vanilla extract
- 2–3 drops of pink food colouring
- 250g good-quality apricot jam
- 225g ready-made marzipan (you can also get it pre-rolled)
- icing sugar, for dusting

- Preheat your oven to 180°C/Gas Mark 4. Line a 20cm square cake tin with baking parchment. There are quite a few ways that you can do this but I've found that the following method used by the Queen of British baking, Mary Berry, works out the simplest. Cut a piece of baking parchment about 5–6cm longer than your tin. Fold the paper into a pleat in the centre then line the base. You want the pleat to be tall and proud along the middle of your tin so it makes two compartments.

- Put the butter, sugar, flour, ground almonds, baking powder, eggs and vanilla extract in a bowl and beat with an electric whisk until the mixture is smooth. It is important your butter is soft to get the batter smooth. Pour half of the mixture into the tin, using a spatula to get it all out. Add a few drops of food colouring to the remaining mixture and combine. Add to the empty half of your tin and level each of the mixtures with a knife, making sure the pleat of baking parchment is as straight as possible. Bake for 30 minutes or until a skewer inserted into the centre comes out clean. Leave the cake to cool in the tin and then tip on to a wire rack.

- Trim the edges of the cake and cut into four equal-sized strips. Lay one pink and one cream strip next to each other and stick them together with the apricot jam. Repeat with the remaining two strips and lay them on top of the first strips with a layer of jam between them. Make sure you lay them the opposite way round to create your Battenberg check. Brush the top of the cake with more jam.

- Roll the marzipan into a rectangle slightly bigger than the sponge and about 0.5cm thick. Invert the cake on to the marzipan then brush the sides of the cake with jam. Carefully roll the cake over the marzipan to cover it, trim the excess marzipan and seal with a little water. Make sure the seal is on the bottom and dust the top of the cake with icing sugar. Serve in slices with a pot of tea.

Opera Cake

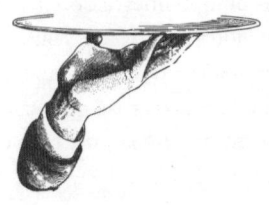

If you have ever walked past a Parisian patisserie and stopped for a minute to admire the window displays, you will be familiar with the Opera Cake. This unusual rectangular slab of chocolate and coffee sponge normally takes centre stage, its angular features making a bold contrast to the whirling meringues or the domes of macaroons and piles of tiny candies. Its mixture of very thin dark and light layers is a thing of immense beauty and represents over three hundred years of dedicated work in the world of patisserie. Although the cake itself was created just 60 years ago, this story begins much earlier than that – in 1682, at the court of King Louis XIV.

Louis de Bourbon, Prince of Condé, was a distant relative of the King and a war hero whose military prowess earned him the title Le Grand Condé. His title gave him a fair income and in his retirement he held lavish fêtes and garden parties at the Château de Chantilly, just north of Paris. Which were attended by artists, clergy and royalty.

This was a time of great pomp in France: the bloody revolution that saw so many heads roll was still a hundred years in the future. Out of Le Grand Condé's kitchens was coming some of the finest food France had to offer. They had become notorious some years earlier after their meticulous former maître d'hôtel François Vatel committed suicide over the late arrival at dinner of some fish. But in 1682 their greatest appeal lay in the work of the pastry chef, Charles Dalloyau. Louis XIV was often present at the Prince's firework fetes and it was on one such occasion that his fine palate and eager appetite took notice of some intricate and particularly petite bread canapés that were on offer.

Louis immediately demanded to meet the man responsible and in the waft of an arm had him installed in his own new home, the Palace of Versailles. Dalloyau worked at Versailles for the rest of his life and three generations of Dalloyau men followed suit. Their name was recognized by the title Officier de Bouche, which translates rather unattractively as 'Officer of the Mouth'. It was the highest title that could be bestowed on any culinary worker and allowed the Dalloyau men to wear swords in the presence of the King – a very rare thing indeed, especially when most people wanted to remove his head from his shoulders. When the revolution came and in 1789 the Palace of Versailles was emptied Jean-Baptiste Dalloyau, the great-great-great-grandson of Charles, was stripped of all titles. He went into business in Paris, setting up the first Dalloyau shop in the rue du Faubourg Saint-Honoré, where it still stands. Saint Honoré, incidentally, is the patron saint of pastry chefs.

In 1903 the Exposition Culinaire hit Paris and it is said that the first Opera-style cake, containing the same layering and sponge components, was displayed here by a chef from a rival pastry shop, Louis Clichy. But it was in 1955 that Cyriaque Gavillon, director of the now very modern Dalloyau business, created the grand gâteau that would make his firm's creations as famous as the name above the shop.

Gavillon wanted to invent a new style of cake. Up till that time, it didn't matter how you filled, topped, iced and stacked your cakes, they almost all shared one characteristic – they were round. Gavillon wanted to change this. He wanted a square cake. Unremarkable as this sounds, it required some courage: it takes a brave man to veer away from the norm in French gastronomy, where the rules laid down over the centuries by chefs such as Carême, Dubois and Escoffier are cherished to this day.

Gavillon also wanted a cake that would allow each bite to reveal all the flavours contained within. So he began to layer very thin sheets of joconde sponge soaked in coffee and garnished with coffee buttercream and chocolate ganache. Although the finished cake was only a few centimetres high the number of layers nearly reached double figures. It was remarkable for its shape, its beauty and its deep, rich flavour. It remained light and delicate and stood with pride in the shop window.

The cake's physical resemblance to the nearby Paris Opera House resulted in Gavillon's wife and co-director Andrée naming it *L'Opéra*. It has come to symbolize the very pinnacle of French skill with pastry and a visit to Dalloyau is on every food tourist's 'to do' list. Only the foolhardy attempt their own. The recipe included here will get you there, but it is up to your own nimble hands to work the magic and create quite possibly the perfect cake.

Opera Cake

This impressive cake understandably adorns many of the patisserie windows in Paris.

Serves 4–6

For the almond sponge
- 2½ tablespoons plain flour
- 75g icing sugar
- 75g ground almonds
- 3 eggs, plus 3 egg whites
- 15g unsalted butter, melted and cooled
- 1 tablespoon caster sugar

For the ganache
- 100g good-quality dark chocolate, finely chopped
- 60ml milk
- 55ml thick cream
- 25g unsalted butter, softened

For the buttercream
- 70g caster sugar
- 1 egg white
- 1 tablespoon instant coffee dissolved in 1 teaspoon boiling water
- 100g unsalted butter, softened

For the coffee syrup
- 1½ tablespoons sugar and 1½ tablespoons instant coffee dissolved in 90ml water

- Preheat the oven to 220°C/Gas Mark 7. Line a 20 x 30cm cake tin with baking parchment. In a large bowl, sift together the flour and icing sugar then add the ground almonds. Mix well. Add the eggs, one at a time, and beat the mixture until pale. Add the melted butter. In a separate bowl beat the egg whites until stiff, then gradually add the sugar and continue beating until stiff peaks are formed. Add a third of the egg whites to the batter, mixing well, then incorporate the rest, folding until just combined. Pour into the cake tin and spread evenly. Bake for 6–8 minutes or until golden and springy to the touch. Loosen the edges with a knife and carefully turn out on to a wire rack covered with a sheet of baking parchment. Leave to cool.

- To make the ganache, put the chopped chocolate in a heatproof bowl. Bring the milk and 30ml of the cream to the boil in a saucepan and pour over the chocolate. Wait 30 seconds, then add the butter and mix until smooth. Leave it to cool to a spreadable consistency.

- To make the buttercream, put the sugar and 3 tablespoons water in a heavy skillet and stir until the sugar is completely dissolved. Boil, without stirring, until the syrup reaches soft-ball stage (116°C–118°C). Beat the egg white in a clean bowl until soft peaks are formed. Continue beating while incorporating the hot sugar syrup until the mixture is cold. Add the coffee mixture and the butter. Beat well until thoroughly combined.

- Divide the sponge into three equal sections (10 x 20cm) and carefully peel off the baking parchment. Soak the first section in a third of the coffee syrup then spread over half of the buttercream. Place the next section of sponge on top, then soak with half the remaining coffee syrup and spread with half of the ganache. Place the last section on top, soak with the remaining coffee syrup and spread with the remaining buttercream, taking care to smooth the surface. Chill until the buttercream is firmly set.

- Melt the remaining ganache in a heatproof bowl set over a saucepan of very hot water. Bring the reserved cream to the boil and incorporate into the ganache. Cool until a smooth, spreadable consistency is obtained and spread over the top of the cake.

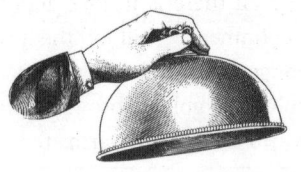

Madeleines

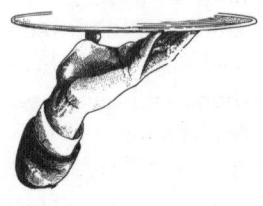

The Madeleine may not be laden with intricate sugar work or balanced on a nest of perfectly baked meringue, but sit it next to a cup of dark black coffee or perch it on the edge of a bowl full of decadent sabayon and it symbolizes all there is to love about French cuisine. It combines the immense skill of the pastry chef to get the génoise sponge light and moist with the precision of the baker to colour it golden brown with a biscuit edge. Madeleines have to be served warm; they do keep, but to get that hit of Parisian perfection they must heat the palm of your hand just a little to let you know they are alive. The name, of course, conjures up images of beautiful French maidens with porcelain skin and dark, brooding eyes. It somehow elevates this already great sponge biscuit to ethereal heights.

Far and away the most famous fan of the Madeleine was the French novelist and essayist Marcel Proust. In his most important work *In Search of Lost Time* or *Remembrance of Things Past* (published in France in seven volumes between 1913 and 1927), he used the Madeleine as an example of something that can evoke a powerful memory instantly, without effort or verbal trigger; its flavour and texture took him immediately to a time long gone, but etched forever into his subconscious. The Madeleine's story, however, begins a good century before Proust gave it literary leanings.

Let's travel back to the luxurious kitchens of one of France's greatest gourmets, the diplomat Charles Maurice de Talleyrand-Périgord. In the early part of the nineteenth century Talleyrand was famous for his gastronomic passion and employed the king of chefs, Marie-Antoine Carême. But it was another chef who would be the instigator of great French pastry, a man who would eventually help refine Carême's talent and one whom many won't have heard of: Jean Avice. Avice was a master of pastry. His shop-window displays of historic buildings made from spun and crafted sugar were works of art, and his creations made Talleyrand's frequent feasts the most celebrated in France.

The fashion of the time was for lavish banqueting tables laden with the whole meal to be exhibited from the start of a feast. Decorative foods held in aspic were the centrepieces of these artistic displays. So it's not a huge leap for the great pastry chef to be tempted to use his scallop-shelled aspic moulds to bake his delicious, light génoise sponge. This is as far as our knowledge goes and it explains only how the cake became centre stage in a Parisian patisserie's window; it gives no clue as to how the Madeleine got its name.

Some food historians believe that the recipe may have existed a half-century earlier and credit a pastry chef called Madeleine Paulmier with its invention; she was supposedly working for King Stanislas Leszczyński, an exiled Pole living in the small town of Commercy in the Duchy of Lorraine. More reliable sources say that the Polish exile was enamoured of a local village baker who shared the same name and fell in love with both her and her shell-shaped cakes. It's also possible that they were made by the nuns from the local convent of St Mary Magdalene. Either way, it happens that Stanislas' daughter Marie was married to King Louis XV of France, so Madeleines were soon on show at the Palace of Versailles and then in Paris itself, becoming a favourite of the French King.

There is, of course, yet another possibility — that a small génoise-like sponge cake in a vague shell shape was in existence throughout the eighteenth century but not widely known. Recipes travel and great chefs are always watching and learning, devising new ways to improve things. A generation after Stanislas and Louis XV, it is perfectly credible that Jean Avice used the tools at his disposal to adapt the Madeleine. There's no doubt that they made beautiful displays and flew out of his shop door, especially fresh from the oven.

Whichever story you believe, once Proust had given words to people's feelings towards Madeleines their place in the pantheon of food greats was assured. Like so many aspects of French cooking their construction is a matter of pride. To get them just right is a sign of immense skill, so it is no wonder they drove Marcel to describe them as 'the little scallop-shell of pastry, so richly sensual under its severe, religious folds'.

What will they make you think about?

Madeleines

Madeleines are a thing of real beauty and to get them right will fill you with satisfaction. For me the difference is in the edges and golden caster sugar helps you get that little biscuit crust that can make or break your Madeleines. You can eat them warm from the oven but they are also delicious with a beaten egg sabayon if you want to turn them into a showpiece dessert.

Makes approx. 12

- 125g unsalted butter, plus extra for greasing
- 100g golden caster sugar
- 40g ground almonds
- 40g plain flour
- 3 large egg whites
- finely grated zest of ½ orange
- salt

- You need to move quite quickly with these steps. Gently melt the butter in a saucepan over a medium heat. Once it starts to foam just a little strain it and set aside.

- Sift the sugar, ground almonds and flour into a bowl. Whisk the egg whites in a separate bowl then fold into the dry mix. Pour in the butter in one stream – it needs to still be warm. Add the orange zest and a little salt – just enough to stop the mixture becoming sickly. Mix until thoroughly combined. Cover the bowl with clingfilm and put in the fridge to chill for at least an hour.

- If you are not using non-stick moulds then butter them and dust with flour to ensure the cakes come out easily. Fill your madeleine moulds with the mixture and return to the fridge for at least 30 minutes.

- Preheat the oven to 180°C/Gas Mark 4.

- Bake for 10–15 minutes or until set and lightly golden brown. Leave to cool slightly on a wire rack for 3–4 minutes, giving you just enough time to put the kettle on and make a cup of coffee to accompany them.

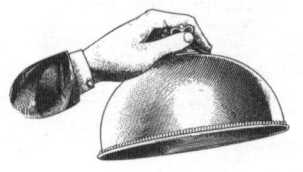

Lamington

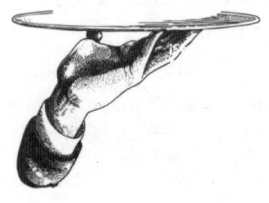

To have a dish named after you must be considered one a life's greatest accolades. However, imagine for a second that the dish that bears your name is one of your least favourite things to eat and when it is wheeled out for you to enjoy at every opportunity you are faced with an awkward and politically damaging encounter. Well, this is exactly what happened to Charles Wallace Alexander Napier Cochrane-Baillie, 2nd Baron Lamington, when in 1901 a small chocolate and coconut cake was chosen as the way in which to celebrate his contribution to the state of Queensland in Australia.

The Lamington is a simple cake, a classic sponge made of butter, eggs and sugar, then rolled in warm chocolate icing and dusted in coconut. It is served in small squares and is now a national icon. Nearly every Australian knows how to make one and New Zealanders even claim it as their own invention (a feature of quite a few Australasian dishes!). Today it is the official National Cake of Australia and has its own National Day – 21 July.

But to go back to Lord Lamington. He became Governor of Queensland in 1896 and had a huge job on his hands. Australia was going through the biggest political change in its history: federation. The six self-governing colonies were merging to form one nation and it was Lamington's task to ensure that Queensland still held its voice within the new federal government.

This meant constant meetings and negotiations, planning, drafting and eventually signing constitutions. As we know from today's politicians, a meeting of any kind in political circles requires a dinner, especially if a real decision is to be made. There were plenty of people who wanted to talk about this new Australia, so it was not unusual to hold a banquet with very little time to prepare.

Last-minute guests have always been a chef's biggest fear and on one occasion it seems that Lord Lamington's French chef, Armand Galland, was caught particularly short: a lack of fresh cream and any fruit made dessert a real problem. How confident he felt about the success of leftover sponge cake rolled in chocolate and dusted in coconut is anybody's guess, but he knew that coconut was an exotic ingredient that would provide a talking point. And talk they did. Almost every guest demanded the recipe to take home that night. The newly born Australian people were fiercely proud of anything they could claim as truly their own and this furry-looking sponge cake was perfect.

The cakes quickly became known as Lamingtons in honour of the Governor; however he never quite embraced them with as much political gusto as perhaps he should have. He even went as far as to describe them as 'bloody poofy woolly biscuits'. But then this is also the man who, during a state visit to the great national park that is named after him, asked his driver to pull over only to take out his gun and shoot a hanging koala out of a tree!

The first recorded recipe for Lamingtons appeared in the *Queenslander* newspaper in 1902, although it didn't use the name. All recipes prior to 1910 describe a whole cake dipped in chocolate and rolled in coconut; the smaller squares evolved later. The connection with Lord Lamington seems first to have appeared in print as late as 1933, in the Perth *Sunday Times* under a column named 'Honourable Mention'.

However, there is a twist in this tale and it comes in the form of recent research by an Australian professor, Maurice French. It seems that a Queensland cookery teacher by the name of Ann Shauer published a recipe for a coconut sponge cake very much like a Lamington in the year 1904.

Ms Shauer was a respected writer and her cookery classes were attended by many local residents, including a certain Lady Lamington. Professor French believes that rather than the Lord's French chef being the creator of Lamingtons, it was the Lady's cookery teacher and that the newly made cake was named in her honour, not her husband's.

These days the Lamington is the ubiquitous fundraising cake, always present at a street party or sold to raise money for a good cause. Its success in Australia could also be down to its ability to survive in the hot, dry climate where other, more buttery batters would suffer. There are many more exotic dishes around in our modern cosmopolitan cuisine, but the Lamington throws you back to a simpler gastronomic time. Australia has come a long way in its brief history, but some things don't change and one of them is the Lamington.

Lamington

I like to make these after baking some other birthday or celebration cakes. Bake off an extra sponge so that you can leave it overnight for your Lamingtons. It will be slightly firmer and won't fall apart when rolled in the chocolate icing and coconut.

Makes approx. 15

For the sponge
- 125g unsalted butter, softened
- 170g caster sugar
- 1 teaspoon vanilla extract
- 2 eggs
- 185g plain flour
- 1¼ teaspoons baking powder
- 125ml milk

For the icing
- 25g unsalted butter, softened
- 95g icing sugar
- 2 tablespoons cocoa powder
- 80ml water, boiled
- 35g shredded coconut

- Preheat the oven to 160°C/Gas Mark 3 and line a 30 x 20cm cake tin with baking parchment.

- To make the icing, melt the butter in a saucepan. Combine the icing sugar, cocoa powder, boiling water and the melted butter in a bowl and whisk them together. Set aside.

- To make the sponge, use an electric whisk to combine the butter, caster sugar and vanilla until light and creamy. Gradually add the eggs then sift in the flour and baking powder and fold in. Stir in the milk.

- Pour the sponge mixture into the cake tin. Bake for 20 minutes or until a skewer inserted into the centre comes out clean.

- Leave the cake to cool slightly in the tin then transfer to a wire rack.

- Top with the icing and dust with the shredded coconut. If you wish, or you are from New Zealand, you could cut the cakes in half and fill with raspberry jam before topping with the chocolate and coconut. Serve cut into squares.

Garibaldi
biscuits

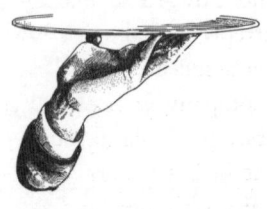

Of all the biscuits in the tin there is one that stands alone and dares to be different. Its two sandwich layers with a filling of squashed currants (hence its popular nicknames of 'squashed fly biscuits' or 'fly cemeteries') are a world apart from a rich tea or a custard cream. It even comes in a sheet for you to separate. For biscuit-lovers it is a hero. It should never be eaten alone, always with a cup of tea, and should never be rushed. Its origin and namesake share these same heroic traits; this is a story of pioneering and endeavour, bravery and risk. So put the kettle on, plump up a cushion and prepare for a tale involving Italian rebels, Tyneside shipbuilders and plenty of biscuits.

Our story begins in 1850, in the borough of Bermondsey, East London. James Peek was a tea merchant – a mildly successful one, too. However, his sons Charles and Edward were not tea-lovers and had no interest in taking over the business. So James hatched a plan to find them something more congenial to do. His niece, Hannah, had married a man called George Frean who, having made his money selling gunpowder, was now milling flour and producing ship's biscuits. When Peek approached him with an offer to join Charles and Edward in managing a new biscuit factory, Frean's entrepreneurial spirit saw an opportunity. He lured in another associate, John Carr, whose family ran a notable biscuit company in Scotland (the Carr's water biscuit proving to be a particular favourite).

It happened that in 1861 Carr was looking for a way to improve a biscuit's sweetness and texture without just adding sugar; dried currants provided him with the perfect solution. Trade with the Americas was bringing in lots of affordable new ingredients and the smallness of the fruit meant it didn't increase the size of the biscuit too much.

Keeping the end product in sheets made storage and transport simple and the biscuits could easily be shipped around the world to emerging markets in Australia and the Far East.

It might seem a little random to name your new confectionery creation after an Italian revolutionary, but let's put this in a geographical and historical perspective. For some time, Giuseppe Garibaldi had been battling his way around the divided Italian regions, trying to throw out foreign rulers (including the King of Naples, who was descended from the French royal family). Having forced the occupying Neapolitan forces to surrender in Sicily in 1860, he set his sights on the mainland and headed for Naples to fight his biggest ever battle. The late arrival of a large force of Piedmontese troops helped him to victory and his dream of a unified nation moved close to realization.

People around the world stood up and took notice of this slick, thick-bearded man. He was already a hero to many people in Britain following a visit to Tyneside in 1854, when his arrival was met with large crowds, celebration and much newspaper coverage. When he finally brought Italy together seven years later the people of Britain were firmly on his side. The Peek, Frean and Co. biscuit company seized the chance to mark his global fame by naming their new biscuit in his honour. Some stories say the connection was inspired by the rather unsavoury practice of some of Garibaldi's hardcore men of soaking stale biscuits in horse's blood to moisten them before eating. A small percentage from the sales of Garibaldi biscuits was sent to Italy to help with the final push towards unification.

Peek, Frean and Co. found even more success soon after, when John Carr created the Pearl biscuit, a simple, flat, almost all-butter biscuit which would become the template for modern biscuit-making. This, combined with the onset of the Franco-Prussian War in 1870, was to set the trio of British biscuiteers up for the rest of their lives. The need for some ten million navy biscuits and the general growth of international trade allowed them to expand to America and Australia, taking their biscuits with them.

The Garibaldi was marketed under different names as far afield as New Zealand and up until 2001 was produced in the States in the 'Golden Fruit' range by the now defunct Keebler Biscuit Company. Today only the United Kingdom still makes a Garibaldi biscuit.

It may be easier to grab a packet from your supermarket shelf, but making your own is well worth it and will give you time to pay thanks to John Carr, the greatest biscuit-maker of them all.

 # Garibaldi biscuits

This is a biscuit that wasn't designed for home construction but it's well worth having a go and whatever happens you can marvel at the great biscuiteers of the past. Their skill and technical prowess have made it possible to remember Italy's great war hero every time we have a biscuit and a pot of tea.

Makes approx. 18

- 100g butter, melted
- 100g icing sugar, sifted
- 100g plain flour
- 100g egg whites
- 200g currants

- In a bowl, mix together the butter, icing sugar and flour until smooth. Slowly add the egg whites, stirring until they are completely incorporated, then fold in the currants. The dough will be quite wet. Place in a small bowl and chill in the fridge for at least an hour.

- Line a shallow baking tin with baking parchment and spread the mixture evenly in the tin. Chill in the fridge for 30 minutes.

- Preheat the oven to 180°C/Gas Mark 4.

- Bake the biscuits for 25–30 minutes or until golden brown. While soft, cut into slices with a sharp knife. Leave to cool – they will keep well stored in an airtight container for a week.

And to Drink...

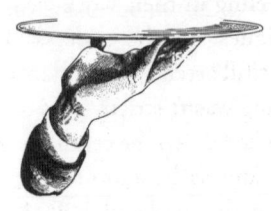

Bellini

Normally a barman would set about creating a drink by getting out his favourite spirits, mixers and fruit, trying them in different ratios to create a flavour he liked and then thinking about garnishes and glasses. The Bellini, however, owes its existence to a rather different motivation – colour.

Throughout the period known as the Renaissance, Venice produced many artists and attracted many others who made their way there to capture the likeness of Italy's beautiful watery city in whatever medium they could. Venetian-born Giovanni Bellini was one such: he revolutionized art in his native city in the fifteenth century. The Renaissance was an extraordinary time, when sculptors, painters, writers, architects and scientists rediscovered the learning of ancient Greece and Rome and sought to express human feeling in their work via a revival of these ideas and techniques. In the process they produced a collection of beautiful artefacts to enhance all our lives.

Cocktail drinking wasn't strictly part of the Renaissance, but its effects travelled down the centuries and made a mark on Giuseppe Cipriani as he adorned the walls of Harry's Bar in Venice with the works of Bellini and his students – including Carpaccio, after whom Giuseppe named that famous beef dish some years later (see page 48).

So, back to the drink. Sometime around 1948 Cipriani decided to create a new cocktail using Italy's famous fizzy nectar, Prosecco. The French had champagne cocktails and he wanted something his people could claim as their own. He wanted it to be sweet, as his customers tended to drink more sweet cocktails than sour, and most importantly he wanted it to be a soft pinky colour to match a robe worn in one of Bellini's paintings. The art galleries of Venice had many examples of the great man's work, but which painting inspired Cipriani's colour choice is not clear; Bellini was fond of light pink garments, so there are quite a few options. My personal favourite is *The Ecstasy of St Francis*, not for its powerful religious echoes and the striking cruciform positioning of the monk – I just like the colour. Cipriani settled on peach juice for his mixer and slowly worked on proportions, much as the great painter would have done, until he found the shade he liked. Thankfully it tasted great too and the Bellini cocktail was born.

At the time Harry's Bar was the watering hole for local socialites and visiting superstars. The Bellini became its signature cocktail during the summer months, when fresh white peaches were available. (It later became a year-round favourite when white peach purée was produced commercially.) In 1985 the Cipriani family made a transatlantic crossing to open their first New York bar, taking the drink with them. These days the Bellini is one of the world's iconic drinks and is even included in the International Bartenders' Association annual cocktail-making competition.

I find it useful to keep a copy of my favourite Bellini painting on the fridge for inspiration.

Bellini

Serves 1

- 50ml white peach purée
- 100ml Prosecco

- Pour the peach purée into the bottom of a chilled champagne flute then gently fill with the Prosecco.

Cosmopolitan

If ever a drink symbolized a specific time it is the bright pink, citric Cosmopolitan. That time was the 1990s. It was the drink to be seen with. In New York people drank Cosmopolitans by the trayload in the elevated Rainbow Room bar inside the Rockefeller Center. One photo of Madonna enjoying a Cosmo on a night out, coupled with the weekly cocktail-drinking adventures of Carrie Bradshaw and her friends in *Sex and the City*, was all it took to make the drink a phenomenon.

Its story begins as recently as 1968. Marketing men for the company Ocean Spray were looking for a way to bring their cranberry juice to the adult market, so on every carton they printed a recipe for a new cocktail called the Harpoon. This consisted of vodka, cranberry juice and lime and it may have lacked finesse, but it was enough to encourage barmen to start experimenting.

Of the number of people who are credited with bringing a cranberry-flavoured cocktail to a wider audience, the main player appears to be a bartender named Cheryl Cook, working in South Beach, Florida, in the late 1970s. She noticed that her customers wanted to be seen drinking something sophisticated like a Martini, but that in fact it was too sour for them. So she decided to create a cocktail that would suit the Miami crowd. She used lemon-infused vodka and triple sec combined with lime for sharpness and sweetened it with just enough cranberry juice to make it pretty. She says she chose the name as a direct link to the magazine *Cosmopolitan*, whose style and design she was trying to reflect.

Cook's role in the history of the Cosmopolitan is constantly disputed – some say she didn't even exist – but one man who can be pinpointed for helping the drink's global domination was John Caine. He came across variations while working the bars of Provincetown, Massachusetts, which in the 1970s was a popular destination among emerging gay communities. Provincetown is not far from one of the main cranberry-producing areas in America, and the Cosmopolitan had become incredibly popular as a way of using the local juice. When Caine left to start his own bar in San Francisco a few years later he took the drink with him.

The Cosmopolitan became widely known in trendy bars in Frisco at a time when its gay population was enjoying a new sexual freedom. People hung out, drinking, smoking and having fun. It was during this time that the drink began to creep into popular culture. The writings of Armistead Maupin described the San Francisco social scene and soon the Cosmo had spread across the country, eventually making its way to New York and into those *Sex and the City* girls' glasses.

The current version of the Cosmopolitan is credited to one of two bartenders, Dale Degroff at the Rainbow Room or Toby Cecchini at the Odeon in Tribeca. Both tweaked Cook's original mix, switching from lime cordial to fresh lime and insisting on Absolut Citron as their vodka of choice. Their changes stuck and Madonna's seal of approval did the rest.

Cosmopolitan

SERVES 1

- 30ml vodka citron
- 15ml Cointreau
- 15ml lime juice
- 15ml cranberry juice
- orange peel, to garnish

- Shake the vodka, Cointreau, lime juice and cranberry juice vigorously in a cocktail shaker with cubes of ice.

- Strain into a martini glass, garnish with a piece of orange peel and serve.

Margarita

Sadly for a cocktail that shares its name (although not spelling) with the equally famous Pizza Margherita, the identity of this Margarita's creator will probably never be known with the same certainty. There are as many versions of its story as there are bars in the world; most tend to agree on one thing though, that the drink was born in Mexico.

The earliest story comes from Tijuana in 1935, where a barman called Danny Herrera is credited with having made the first Margarita for a lady called not Margarita, but Marjorie King. Marjorie was a Ziegfeld Follies girl, one of the exotic dancing troupes which were taking over Broadway with their high-kicking, minimally clothed routines. She was apparently allergic to any alcohol except tequila but hated the taste, so Danny solved her problem for her. Margarita is the Spanish equivalent to Marjorie. A simple story.

Move on a few years to 1941 and a little down the road to the town of Ensenada, where a bartender called Don Carlos Orozco was mixing the drinks at Hussong's Cantina. Opened back in 1892 by a young German named Johan Hussong, it had quickly become the favourite watering hole for anyone able to escape across the border. In true bar-talk style, the story goes that one day Hussong was travelling in the area when his coach crashed, leaving his companion badly injured. They sought refuge in Ensenada's only bar. The next day the owner proceeded to murder his wife and was carted off to jail, asking Johan to look after things while he was gone. The companion recovered and returned to his family and the owner never returned, leaving Johan with his own business.

So one quiet afternoon in October 1941, Don Carlos had one customer, Margarita Henkel – the daughter of the German ambassador to Mexico, no less. He was playing around with new flavours and different alcohols and she was a willing guinea pig. She loved the heady citric bite of this new super juice. It needed a name, so he called it after her.

Another simple story.

Yet another version puts the Margarita across the Mexican border in Texas, and involves iconic singer Peggy Lee, but this is getting very tenuous. Lee was a frequent visitor to the Balinese Room in Galveston, where in 1948 barman Santos Cruz created the drink in her honour, again naming it after the Spanish version of her full name. The truth is probably neither as romantic nor as simple as any of these stories.

Prior to the 1940s several cocktails were popular in different forms in different parts of America. One such was the Daisy, which consists of a heavily distilled liqueur shaken with a citrus-based liqueur and some sugar. The most popular in the US was the Brandy Daisy. Over the border in Mexico brandy was unavailable, so many bars served it with the most common alcohol down south, tequila. There are records of the Tequila Daisy being drunk all over America as early as 1936. The *Syracuse Herald*, the *Albuquerque Journal* and even *Time* magazine mention it as a popular drink at the time. And the Spanish for Daisy is, you guessed it, Margarita!

Just don't ask me why it was called a Daisy.

Margarita

Serves 1

- wedge of lime
- a handful of sea salt, finely ground
- 50ml tequila
- 50ml Cointreau
- 50ml lime juice

- Rub the rim of the glass with the lime then dip the glass in the salt to coat the rim.
- Fill the glass with crushed ice. Combine the remaining ingredients in a cocktail shaker.
- Pour into the ice-filled glass and stir to combine. Serve immediately.

Martini

If you were ever looking for a drink that was destined to exist, it would have to be the Martini. Its journey through the world's cocktail bars has seen it evolve into the most popular and best-known cocktail ever. It even survived Prohibition, the period of enforced sobriety between 1920 and 1933 in the United States. In fact it flourished during this time, when alcohol was illegal and people had to make gin in bathtubs. Drinkers had to be creative about how they got their liquor and gin was the easiest to produce. But nobody wanted to feel they were drinking something that had been born in a bathtub – they wanted something altogether more sophisticated.

Folklore places the Martini's early roots in a drink named a Martinez, served in the Occidental Hotel in the town of Martinez, California. The hotel was next to a ferry terminal where people would wait and take a drink as the ferry went back and forth (or, according to a variation on the story, it may have been in San Francisco, where people waited for the ferry to Martinez). The creation of the Martinez is now something of an early American myth, with a young gold digger back in 1870 placing a nugget on the bar and demanding something special from the barman, Julio Richelieu. The Martinez was the result: a combination of two parts sweet vermouth to one part gin. However, the *Oxford English Dictionary* has two Italians named Martini and Rossi down as the inspiration for the name at least: Alessandro Martini had been importing vermouth into the United States since 1863 and its popularity had spread across the country and the world.

As Prohibition kicked in people still had easy access to gin, and if they knew the right people they could get their hands on vermouth, so the Martini was born; it became a dryer, sleeker drink, and from then on the fun began. You could mix yours to exactly the balance of gin and vermouth you liked – the less vermouth, the 'drier' the Martini. After the end of Prohibition, with good-quality gin freely available again, the Martini could be made to a very high standard. It was in the 1940s that the switch from sweet to dry vermouth began to occur. By the 1970s the Martini's star was fading a little as people shifted to lighter drinks like spritzers and more intricate cocktails, but it is still considered a classic.

These days people add vodka (something that evolved in the 1950s) and other alcohols (James Bond famously adds the aperitif Kina Lillet to his in *Casino Royale*, also from the 1950s), but purists will say that there should be only two ingredients in a Martini – gin and vermouth. The only other addition may be a garnish such as an olive or a pickled onion (although this is called a Gibson). Some people even make a 'dirty Martini' by including the olive brine.

Martini

Serves 1

- 50ml gin
- 15ml dry vermouth
- olive, to garnish

- Pour the ingredients into a mixing glass with a couple of ice cubes. Stir well.
- Strain into a chilled martini cocktail glass.
- Garnish with a pitted olive. If you like yours dry then adjust the ratio with less vermouth.

Piña Colada

Some words should never be translated. Piña Colada literally means 'strained pineapple', which is neither appetizing nor memorable. Its story is thankfully much more colourful than the creamy white drink itself. There are tales harking back to the 1800s and a pirate named Roberto Cofresí, who used to supply it to his weary men to boost their morale as they spent long years at sea. According to folklore, Cofresí was a Puerto Rican Robin Hood, targeting only rich American ships to spread their goods around the poor islanders of Haiti and Puerto Rico. Or, as is the way with stories about pirates, he may have been a heartless killer. Either way, his link to the invention of the Piña Colada should be taken with a good pinch of salt or a squeeze of lime! Legend states that he took the recipe with him to Davy Jones's locker in 1825, so no one will ever know for sure.

Printed recipes for the cocktail date back to the 1920s, including one in *Travel* magazine that described 'the juice of a perfectly ripe pineapple – a delicious drink in itself – rapidly shaken up with ice, sugar, lime and Bacardi rum in delicate proportions. What could be more luscious, more mellow and more fragrant?' But we have to wait until 1950s Puerto Rico to get the coconut-flavoured drink we know and love today.

The main difference between the modern-day Piña Colada and our pirate friend's version is the use of coconut cream. You may not have been aware until this moment how pivotal Puerto Rico was in the technological advancement of the creaming of coconuts, but the process was developed at the University of Puerto Rico by Ramón López Irizarry in 1949. He eventually commercialized it and coconut cream hit the streets as a product called Coco López. It was this that Ramón 'Monchito' Marrero, a young bartender at the Caribe Hilton's Beachcomber Bar in San Juan, used to create one of the most iconic drinks in the cocktail world.

The hotel was becoming increasingly popular with high-profile celebrity guests from both Europe and America, including the actress Gloria Swanson. The management wanted a signature drink on which to build their reputation. Monchito rose to the challenge and after three intense months of research and practice the Piña Colada was born on 15 August 1954, using Puerto Rican coconut cream. The drink was a huge success; the sweet, punchy flavours perfectly balanced the acidity of the pineapple. It could be served straight with a slice of fruit or you could go the whole hog and serve it in a pineapple for full theatrical effect. By 1978 three million Piña Coladas had been sold at the hotel; Monchito was rewarded with a grand ceremony and Puerto Rico declared the Piña Colada its national drink.

The cocktail's popularity has stretched across the world, where it has sometimes been labelled uncool. However, some things defy fashion trends and there is nothing like a freshly strained Piña Colada to transport you to the azure sea-swept beach bars of the Caribbean.

It traditionally comes with a Maraschino cherry as a garnish. Personally I say leave it out.

Piña Colada

Serves 1

- 75ml white rum
- 50ml coconut cream
- 50ml pineapple juice
- pineapple slice, to garnish

- Pour all of the ingredients into a blender along with enough crushed ice to fill a serving glass and blend thoroughly until smooth.

- Pour back into your serving glass through a strainer and top with a straw and a piece of pineapple.

Mint Julep

The Mint Julep is a heady mix of bourbon, sugar and mint and is most strongly associated with America's Deep South, but early writings suggest that whiskey may not have been the initial inspiration. The first mention of a julep is from around the 1700s in Carolina, where a sweetened alcoholic concoction was drunk before breakfast to help fight off malaria. The first printed recipe is in a book called *Travels of Four and a Half Years in the United States of America* by John Davis. Published in 1803, it describes a drink named the Old White using 'a dram of spirituous liquor that has mint steeped in it'.

The name julep derives from an Arabic term 'gulab', which can refer to any sweet thing but is most often used to describe a way of sweetening medicine. In the East the sweet thing used was often rose water, but as it migrated west this floral flavour was switched for the indigenous mint. According to drinks historian Chris Morris julep became popular in the agricultural belt in the southeastern states and was consumed very much in the way coffee is today.

It was in the 1800s that the drink became forever associated with horse racing. In 1816 the *Kentucky Gazette* refers to several julep cups being competed for among local horse riders. The farmers of Kentucky had two great hobbies: racing wild horses and distilling whiskey from their corn crops. At that time Kentucky was on the frontiers of the known world and the range of things to do was less varied than on, say, the boulevards of Paris. The corn whiskey became known as bourbon and made an excellent companion to the home-grown mint.

These days most Mint Juleps are consumed on one particular day at one particular place: the Churchill Downs racecourse, Kentucky, on Derby Day. The Kentucky Derby is one of America's great sporting occasions and is named after the Epsom Derby in England. On 17 May 1875, in front of an estimated crowd of 10,000 people, a field of 15 three-year-old horses contested the first Kentucky Derby. It was run over the same distance as its British cousin (about 2.5km) before finding its own length (just over 2km) some years later. A colt named Aristides, trained by Ansel Williamson, won that day.

In 1938 a new tradition started as patrons were offered a Mint Julep in a silver cup to toast the horses at the start of the race. Superstition and horse racing make frequent bedfellows, so once they had a ritual they stuck to it and Mint Juleps have been sold at the start of the Kentucky Derby ever since. These days 120,000 Mint Juleps can be consumed at the track bars during the two-day race meeting, and they are all made from the course's own mint garden, planted in 1875.

Mint Julep's fame spread out from Kentucky as tourists came and went. Stories of betting success would be told while mixing the famous Kentucky cocktail. It may never reach the giddy heights of the Martini or the Margarita in terms of popularity, but true Kentuckians say that when a julep is made properly you can hear angels sing. Go on, have a listen!

Mint Julep

Serves 1

- 60ml bourbon whiskey
- 1 teaspoon icing sugar
- 4 fresh mint sprigs, plus extra to garnish

- Muddle the mint leaves, icing sugar and 2 teaspoons water in a Collins glass. Be careful not to break the leaves up or they become bitter.

- Fill the glass with crushed ice and pour over the bourbon.

- Top with more ice and garnish with a mint sprig. Serve with a straw.

Negroni

The Negroni is one of those cocktails that suffer from a bright colour. Connoisseurs of hard liquor tend to prefer a clear tipple, but they shouldn't be put off trying this one. The Negroni's strength lies in its flavour: despite its pinky-orange hue, it isn't in the least bit sweet; the dry bitterness and the hint of citrus make it grown-up and moreish. In Italy Negronis are always made on the rocks with a slice of orange, but this may be switched for orange peel as you travel the world.

The origins of cocktails are notoriously hard to trace, as their very nature does not help anyone involved in creating them to remember much the following day. What we do know about Negroni is that it was created for Count Camillo Negroni, who used to frequent a bar called Caffè Casoni in Florence at the beginning of the twentieth century. Most cocktail fans at the time were drinking Americanos, which were made from Campari, sweet vermouth and soda. The Americano had been popular since around 1860, when Gaspari Campari founded a company to produce his eponymous liquor. Campari had his own bar in Milan in which to perfect his drinks and the Americano was probably his most famous invention.

Back to our Count, who in about 1918 was having a particularly bad day. He asked Fosco Scarselli, the barman at Caffè Casoni, to make his Americano a little stronger than usual. Fosco duly obliged, swapping the soda for gin, and the Negroni was born. In his book *Sulle Tracce del Conte: La Vera Soria del Cocktail Negroni* (*On the Tracks of the Count: the True Story of the Negroni Cocktail*), Luca Picchi notes that Fosco added the now essential slice of orange, instead of the more common lemon, to mark the creation of something new.

The drink grew in popularity among the sophisticated cocktail-drinking set. Orson Welles reported enjoying one while making *Black Magic* in Rome in 1947, saying, 'The bitters are excellent for your liver, the gin is bad for you. They balance each other.' Ian Fleming was partial to them, too, and the first cocktail James Bond drinks in *Casino Royale*, published in 1953, is a Negroni.

The Count developed a commercial version which he sold in bottle form and which is still available today. Caffè Casoni shut shortly after 1919 and Scarselli eventually found a new home at the Ugolino Golf Club near Florence. These days you will find many Negroni-inspired creations such as the Negroni Sbagliato or the 'wrong Negroni', which replaces the gin with Prosecco, or the Negroski, which switches the gin for vodka.

Negroni

Serves 1

- 30ml gin
- 30ml Campari
- 30ml sweet vermouth (red)
- orange twist, to garnish

- Stir the ingredients in a mixing glass with a long spoon, strain into an ice-filled double rocks glass and garnish with the orange peel.

Sidecar

In a way cocktail-making is much more akin to pastry than to other kinds of cooking. It's all about ratios; the amount of each liquor or mixer and how it compares to the others in the blend is vital to the taste of the finished product. It also helps the drinks travel from bar to bar and from country to country without any part of the flavour being lost in translation. The Sidecar is a drink that has been suitably named, as over its history it has travelled many miles and has earned its place as one of the iconic cocktails.

In America in the mid-nineteenth century cocktails were largely limited to whiskey- and brandy-based mixes like the Old Fashioned and the Brandy Daisy, but as improvements in distillation processes gave barmen a wider variety of better-quality products to work with, they began to develop their drink-making skills. New concoctions heavy with bitter flavours appeared alongside the sweet and sour. Citrus-based liqueurs emerged from other countries and the world began to trade the contents of its drinks cabinets. The Brandy Daisy had already spawned the Margarita on its way to Mexico and when it made it to Paris it became the Sidecar.

The story goes that one unnamed American army captain would travel to a small Paris bar every night in a sidecar driven by a private from his platoon. The first drink he ordered was always a heady mix of zesty orange and heart-warming cognac to thaw him out from the chilly ride. The cocktail became known as a Sidecar in honour of the captain and his method of transport.

Different versions dispute which bar he frequented – the Ritz Hotel in Paris claims it was theirs, while some argue it was the tiny Harry's Bar in the Opera district, but perhaps it just became famous here. Harry's had opened as the New York Bar in 1911 and was home to many expatriate Americans from all walks of life. It was owned by a former star jockey named Tod Sloan, but working behind the bar was Harry MacElhone. Whether or not he invented the Sidecar, the bar – which he bought and renamed in 1923 – became synonymous with them. In 1922 MacElhone published a book called *Harry's ABC of Mixing Cocktails*, which contained a Sidecar recipe. Early printings cited the creator as Pat McGarry of the London Buck's Club. However, later editions claim it was MacElhone himself and that MacGarry merely introduced the drink to London.

Like its Venetian namesake, Harry's Bar became one of the great cocktail landmarks. Many tourists travelled to it to sample both the Sidecar and the White Lady mixed to their original recipes. And before we leave Harry's saloon-style doors we must credit it with one other great cocktail invention – the Bloody Mary.

In 1921, a group of friends led by barman Pete Petiot mixed vodka with tomato juice and a little hit of Tabasco. One of them declared that the drink resembled his girlfriend during one of her performances in a cabaret around the corner. The cabaret's name was *Bucket of Blood* and the girl's name was Mary.

These days Sidecars are a little Old Fashioned (excuse the pun), but they are still perfect after a brisk winter's walk through Paris's beautiful boulevards.

Sidecar

Serves 1

- caster sugar
- 40ml cognac
- 25ml Cointreau
- 15ml lemon juice
- lemon twist, to garnish

- Chill a cocktail glass and dip it into the caster sugar so the rim of the glass is coated.

- Pour the ingredients into a cocktail shaker half full of ice cubes and shake well.

- Pour into your glass and garnish with the lemon peel.

Ramos Gin Fizz

This is a drink that you need the time to wait for. Also known as a Ramos Fizz or New Orleans Fizz, it takes around 12 minutes to shake it together and whisk air into the egg whites to bind the aromatics to the alcohol, but boy is it worth it. The zing from all the citrus fruit coupled with the fun, foamy nature of the drink make this one of life's rib-tickling experiences.

The buzzing cocktail bars of America in the 1880s are the birthplace of all fizz cocktails, their central ingredient being soda water. However, it was New Orleans that took them to its heart and made them famous. The first printed recipe for a gin fizz appeared in Jerry Thomas's *Bartenders Guide* in 1887. It contained six recipes.

It was in 1888 that a New Orleans bartender named Harry C Ramos invented the fizz variety that bears his name. He mixed it in his bar, the Imperial Cabinet Saloon on Gravier Street. At first he named the new drink after his home city, but it quickly became known as the Ramos Gin Fizz in honour of its creator. By 1915 Ramos had moved operations across the road to the Stag, which features in Stanley Clisby Arthur's 1937 book *Famous New Orleans Drinks and How to Mix 'Em*: 'The corps of busy shaker boys behind the bar was one of the sights of the town during Mardi Gras carnival in 1915.' The Ramos Gin Fizz was now part of New Orleans bar culture. Ramos kept the recipe top secret until Prohibition was brought in in 1920; then in an altruistic move he distributed it freely to avoid the drink slipping into extinction.

The mixture of orange flower water and egg white was so popular with the citizens of New Orleans that in 1935 Senator Huey P Long, former Governor of Louisiana, demanded that a bartender from his home town accompany him on a trip to New York. (Prohibition was over by then, but only just.) That way he could still have his beloved drink and also help train the mixologists of the Big Apple how to make them. The Museum of the American Cocktail – which is, inevitably, located in New Orleans – contains newsreel of this event should you wish to see for yourselves.

These days there may be trendier or more brightly coloured drinks, people may even have concerns over raw egg, but if you're brave enough to take the plunge you will be transported straight back to the very beginning of the cocktail years and enter into the spirit of a city that was once so full of life. Raise your glass and pray that New Orleans will find its mojo again, so that drinks like the Ramos Gin Fizz are no longer things of the past but very much of the future!

Ramos Gin Fizz

Serves 1

- 50ml gin
- 30ml single cream
- juice of ½ lemon
- juice of ½ lime
- 1 egg white
- 1 teaspoon fine caster sugar
- 1 teaspoon orange flower water
- 2 drops of vanilla extract
- a dash of soda water

- Add all the ingredients to a cocktail shaker in the order they are listed except the soda water. Add a handful of lightly crushed iced and shake well. You need long shakes as it takes a little while to get the egg white to foam. If you are worried about raw egg white then you can buy it pasteurized and pre-separated.

- Pour into a whiskey sour glass, which is fairly tall and top up with chilled soda water. Be careful with your quantities as this drink is a fine balance between sweet and bitter.

Tom Collins

This simple and refreshing drink made from gin, lemon juice, sugar and soda owes its name to one of the most despised men in New York. For a short time at the end of the nineteenth century the Tom Collins was the most popular cocktail in the city and the man after whom it was named was a topic of conversation all the way from Wall Street to the Bronx. Tom Collins was an unscrupulous man; he was jealous and mean-spirited. He spread rumours about people and caused consternation and anger. He was all these things and more, but most important of all he didn't actually exist.

In 1874 the New York press reported a practical joke that was sweeping the city. People were stopping each other in the street with news of a malicious rumourmonger. He would apparently sit in bars and taverns, then launch into tirades about all manner of people. Luckily for those he spoke about, their friends would immediately rush to tell them what Tom Collins was saying and advise them to find him quickly. 'Have you seen Tom Collins?' became the question on everyone's lips. Newspapers ran stories covering sightings of the most wanted man in America. As far away as Ohio, the *Steubenville Daily Herald* reported that the hoax caused 'frantic young men to rush wildly through the streets of the city on Saturday hunting for the libelous Tom Collins'.

By 1876 the flames had died down and sightings of Tom Collins had been reduced almost to zero. At the time, the man who became known as 'the father of American mixology', a barman called Jerry Thomas, was preparing the latest edition of his, and the world's, first all-inclusive book of cocktails. *Bar-Tender's Guide: How to Mix Drinks or the Bon Vivant's Companion*, first published in 1862, became the textbook of mixology and is still in print today, some 150 years later. Although there is no proof that Thomas invented the Tom Collins or named it in honour of the great hoax, this seems to be the only feasible explanation – that the greatest drinks-maker in America saw an opportunity to tap into the Zeitgeist with a new drink.

By 1878 the popularity of the Tom Collins had spread to the point where O H Byron's *Modern Bartender's Guide* described it as 'a favourite drink in demand everywhere'. However, with the arrival of Prohibition in the 1920s, it drifted out of fashion, only to resurface some years later when American-style bars were appearing in London, Paris, Rome and all over. By this time the Tom Collins was included in nearly all the bartenders' guides and had entered the global vocabulary of drinking.

With the passage of time, new and slightly muddled histories had appeared. One claimed that a headwaiter named John Collins had a whisky cocktail named after him in a London hotel, but that this was renamed after the advent of a new brand of Old Tom Gin. However, the first written record of a John Collins comes from the 1891 edition of Thomas's *Bartender's Guide*, which also contained a recipe for a Tom Collins. So it seems likely that the two drinks existed simultaneously, rather than merging, as this London myth suggests.

Tom Collins

Serves 1

- 1 tablespoon sugar syrup
- juice of 1 medium lemon
- 125ml gin (such as Plymouth or London)
- soda water

- Stir all the ingredients except for the soda water together in a Tom Collins glass and add four ice cubes.

- Top with soda water, stir again, and serve immediately.

Conversion chart

WEIGHTS	MEASUREMENTS	LIQUIDS
5g .... ¼oz	2.5mm .... ⅛in	15ml .... ½fl oz
15g .... ½oz	5mm .... ¼in	25ml .... 1fl oz
20g .... ¾oz	1cm .... ½in	50ml .... 2fl oz
25g 1oz	1.5cm .... ¾in	75ml .... 3fl oz
50g 2oz	2.5cm 1in	100ml .... 3½fl oz
65g 2½oz	3.5cm 1½in	125ml .... 4fl oz
75g 3oz	5cm 2in	150ml .... ¼ pint
125g 4oz	6cm 2½in	175ml .... 6fl oz
150g 5oz	7cm 3in	200ml .... 7fl oz
175g 6oz	10cm 4in	250ml .... 8fl oz
200g 7oz	12cm 5in	275ml .... 9fl oz
250g 8oz	15cm 6in	300ml .... ½ pint
275g 9oz	18cm 7in	325ml .... 11fl oz
300g 10oz	20cm 8in	350ml .... 12fl oz
325g 11oz	23cm 9in	375ml .... 3fl oz
375g 12oz	25cm 10in	400ml .... 4fl oz
400g 13oz	28cm 11in	450ml .... ¾ pint
425g 14oz	30cm 12in	475ml .... 16fl oz
450g 14½oz	33cm 13in	500ml .... 17fl oz
475g 15oz		575ml .... 18fl oz
500g 1lb		600ml .... 1 pint
625g 1¼lb	**SPOONS**	750ml .... 1¼ pints
750g 1½lb		900ml .... 1½ pints
875g 1¾lb	1tsp 5g	1 litre .... 1¾ pints
1kg 2lb	1tbsp 15g	1.2 litres .... 2 pints
1.25kg .... ½lb	1tsp 5ml	1.5 litres .... 2½ pints
1.5kg 3lb	1tbsp 15ml	1.8 litres .... 3 pints
1.75kg 3½lb		2 litres .... 3½ pints
2kg 4lb		2.5 litres .... 4 pints
		2.75 litres .... 5 pints
		3.6 litres .... 6 pints

Index

Ajaib, Mohammed 87
Alaska, US 200
Alciatore, Antoine and Jules 133–5
Alexander I of Russia 56, 189
American War of Independence 43
Anderson, Jean *The American Century Cookbook* 74
Antoine's, New Orleans 133–4
Appert, Nicolas 109–11
apples: 19–23, 187–91, 217–21
Arthur, Stanley Clisby *Famous New Orleans Drinks* 227, 277
Artichoke Benedict 39
Ashley, Diana *Where to Dine* 62
Astor, Caroline Schermerhorn 19
aubergines: 175–9
Aviator Salad 14
Avice, Jean 236–7

Bailly, Sylvain 55
Barrymore, Ethel 32–3
Béchamel, Marquis Louis de 127, 128
beef: 49–53, 55–9, 61–5, 67–71, 73–7, 254
Beethoven, Ludwig van 58
Bellini, Giovanni 50, 253–4
Bellini, Vincenzo *Norma* 175–6
Bennett, Arnold 146–7
Birmingham balti restaurants 85–7
Blangé, Paul 193, 194–5
Bloody Mary 275
Blumenthal, Heston 38
Bogart, Humphrey 74
Bonaparte, Napoleon 55–6, 58, 67, 97–101, 110–11, 145
Borgia, Lucrezia 169–70
bread: 31–5, 43–7, 163–7, 187–91
Brennan, Owen 193–5

Brière, Charles 61
Byron, O H *Modern Bartender's Guide* 281

Café Anglais, Paris 157–8
Café de Paris, Monte Carlo 205–6
Café Royal, London 206
Caffè Casoni, Florence 271, 272
Caine, John 257
Campari, Gaspari 271
Cardini, Caesar 13–15
Carême, Marie-Antoine 55–6, 79, 157, 188–9, 218, 235
French sauces 127, 128
meringue 199
Carlton, London 116, 211, 212
Carnot, Sadi 38
Carpaccio, Vittore 50, 253
Carr, John 247–9
Cavallero, Gene 74
Cecchini, Toby 257
Chaplin, Charlie 44, 49
Charlotte Russe 188–9
Charlotte, Queen 188
Charpentier, Henri 74, 205–9
cheese: 38, 43–7, 127–31, 139–43, 163–7, 175–9
Chez Marie, Paris 140
chicken: 25–9, 67, 91–5, 97–101, 103–7, 109–13
Child, Julia 15, 63, 81, 99, 141, 158, 219
Choron, Alexandre 121–5
Cipriani, Giuseppe 49–53, 253–5
Claiborne, Craig 38
coconut cream 266
Cofresi, Roberto 265
Collinet, Jean Louis François 121
Condé, Prince of 97, 98, 229–30
Cook, Cheryl 256–7

corned beef	39, 44, 45
Coward, Noël	49
cranberry juice	256–7
Cubbison, Harry and Sophie	33

D'Oyly Carte, Richard 115–16
Dalloyau, Charles 229–30
Dalloyau, Jean Baptiste 230
Degroff, Dale 257
Delmonico's, New York 37–8, 140, 200
Deslions, Anna 158
Dickens, Charles 38
Ding Baozhen 103–5
Dinner of the Three Emperors 158
Dorchester, London 146
Dubois, Urbain 79–81, 230
Dugléré, Adolphe 157–9
Dumas, Alexandre *Great Dictionary of Cuisine* 158
Dunand (Napoleon's chef) 97–9

Edward, Prince of Wales 205–6
eggs: 13–17, 25–9, 37–41, 39, 145–9
also see meringue
Eisenhower, Dwight D 165
El Floridita club, Havana 141
Elizabeth II 91–2
Elizabeth Petrovna of Russia 109–10
Escoffier, Auguste 31–5, 74, 93, 115–19, 146, 205–9,
Le Guide Culinaire 73, 81, 117, 206
Esposito, Raffaele 164

Farmer, Fannie *Boston Cooking-School Cook Book* 39, 201
Ferdinand IV of Naples 163
Fields, W C 14
Fleming, Ian *Casino Royale* 263, 272
Fokine, Michel 181

Ford, Gerald 117
Foster, Richard 194
Franco-Prussian war 121–3, 211, 249
Frean, George 247
French style of dining 79–80

Gable, Clark 14
Garibaldi, Giuseppe 169, 177, 248–9
Gavillon, Cyriaque 230–1
George III 188
George, Prince Regent (George IV) 55
Gibbon, Edward 43–4
grapes: 19–23, 115–19

Ham: 37–41, 44
Harris, Richard 187–8
Harry's Bar, Paris 275
Harry's Bar, Venice 49–51, 254
Hemingway, Ernest *Across the River and into the Trees* 51
Henri IV of France 121
Henry VIII 68, 187
Hitchcock, Alfred 49
Holbein, Hans 187
Hôtel de Paris, Monte Carlo 201
Hume, Rosemary 92–3

Ice cream: 74, 193–7, 200–3
Indian food 85–7
Irizzary, Ramón López 266
Ivanov, Ivan 26

Jardin d'Acclimatation, Paris 122

Kentucky Derby, US 269
Keogh, Lawrence 64
Kipling Cakes 225
Kulakofsky, Reuben 44–5
Kurti, Nicholas 201

La Varenne, François Pierre de
Le Cuisinier Français 128
Larousse Gastronomique 61, 98, 129, 207
Latry, François 152
Le Durand, Paris 129
Le Gavroche, London 181
Le Tour d'Argent, Paris 158
Le Voisin, Paris 122–3
Leith, Prue 93
Leszczyński, Stanislas 236–7
Lobster Newberg 140
London theatres 116–17
Long, Huey P 278
Louis Clichy, Paris 230
Louis of Battenberg, Prince 223–4
Louis XIV of France 127, 207, 229–30
Louis XV of France 236–7
Lyons Corner Houses 224–5

MacElhone, Harry 275
MacPherson, John 62
Madonna 256, 257
Marengo, battle of 97–9
Margherita of Italy 164
Marquis, Frederick, 151–3
Marrero, Ramón 'Monchito' 266
Martini, Alessandro 263
Martoglio, Nino 176
Massialot, François 181
Maupin, Armistead 257
Maxim's, Paris 218–19
Mazzei, Francesco 172
McGarry, Pat 275
Melba, Dame Nellie 31–5, 211–13
meringue: 28, 181–5, 200–3
Messager, André *Véronique* 116–17
Mocenigo, Countess Amalia Nani 50
Molokhovets, Elena 62
Montagu, John, 4th Earl of Sandwich 43–4
Monte Carlo 201, 205, 211

Mornay, Duke Philippe de 127
Morris, Chris 168
Moscow restaurants 25–6, 206
muffins: 37–41
Museum of the American Cocktail, New Orleans 278
mushrooms: 61–567–71, 73–7, 97–101

Napoleon III of France 121
Negroni, Count Camillo 271
Nixon, Richard 69, 117

Olivier, Lucien 25–6
Orléans, Prince Philippe, Duke of 212
Orloff, Alexey Fyodorovich 79–80
Oxford Companion to Food, The 98
Oxford English Dictionary 262–3

Pastrami 43, 44
Paulmier, Madeleine 236
Pavillon Henri IV, Paris 121
Pavlova, Anna 181–5
peaches: 32, 211–15, 253–5
Pearl biscuits 248–9
Peek, Frean & Co. 248–9
Peek, James 247
Petiot, Pete 275
Picchi, Luca 272
Pickering, Harry 49
Porter, Cole 19
potatoes: 157–61, 151–5
Prohibition, US 13, 262–3, 277–8, 281
Proust, Marcel *À la recherche du temps perdu* 235, 237
Provincetown, Massachusetts 257
puff pastry: 67–71, 217–21

Ramos, Harry C 277–9
Ranhofer, Charles 37–9, 140, 200–1
raspberries: 32, 211–15

rationing, World War II 146, 151–3
Rector, George *Rector Cook Book* 21
Redoux, Jean 207
Reichenberg, Suzanne 206–7
Reuben, Arnold 44
Riccardo, Ric 165
Richelieu, Julio 262
Ritz Hotel, Paris 116, 275, 211
Ritz, César 115–16, 121, 211
Robespierre, Maximilien 139, 141
Rockefeller Center, the Rainbow Room, New York 257
Rockefeller, John D 37, 134
Roosevelt, Theodore 37, 206
Rossini, Gioachino Antonio 56–7
Rothschild, James Meyer de 14, 56, 79
Roux, Albert 181
Rowe, Silvena 112
Russian style of dining 80

Sachse, Herbert 182
Saint Laurent, Yves 14
Salad Olivier 25–9
sandwiches: 43–7
Sardou, Victorien *Thermidor* 139–40
Sargeant, Mark 118
sauces: 9, 37–41, 79, 121–5, 127–31
Savoy, London 115–16, 145–7, 152, 206, 207, 211–12
Scarselli, Fosco 271–2
Schimmel, Charles 45
Seward, William H 200
Sewell, Ike 165
Sex and the City 256, 257
Siegel, Bugsy 20
Simpson, Wallis 14
Sinatra, Frank 74
Sloan, Tod 275
smoked haddock: 145–9, 157
Spry, Constance 91–3

strawberries: 183
Stroganoff, Count Grigory 61–2
Stroganoff, Count Pavel 61
Swanson, Gloria 266
Swift, Jonathan 133
Szechuan peppercorns: 103–7

Talleyrand, Charles 55, 235–6
Tatin, Stéphanie and Caroline 217–19
Tesla, Nikola 20
Thomas, Jerry *Bar-Tenders Guide* 277, 281
Thompson, Benjamin 199
tomatoes: 175–9, 163–7
Tschirky, Oscar *The Cook Book* 20–1
Twain, Mark 37

Uxelles, Marquis d' 128

Vatel, François 229
Veal Marengo 99
vegetables: 151–5
Virlogeux, Jean Baptiste 146
Voiron, Joseph 129

Wagner, Richard *Lohengrin* 211
Waldorf=Astoria Hotel, New York 19–20, 38
Waters, Elsie and Doris 152
Welles, Orson 49, 272
Wellington, Arthur Wellesley, 1st Duke of 67–8
Wilde, Oscar 37
William I of Prussia 80, 158
Wilson, Woodrow 206
Wolseley, London 64

Acknowledgements

A book is more than just a collection of words. So many people have been involved in producing what you are now holding in your hands.

Thank you to some of the best chefs in Britain for their help and donation of recipes especially Lawrence Keogh, Mark Sargeant, Francesco Mazzei and Silvena Rowe.

I owe a huge debt of gratitude to James Martin whom I had the pleasure of working with for over a decade and who has written the marvellous foreword to this book.

I wrote this book many years ago and I want to thank Lucy Pessell and Tim Leng at Octopus Books for digging into their crates to pull it out, dust it off so beautifully and bring it back to the world. Without them I wouldn't have had the chance to look again at some truly wonderful stories.

I am blessed to have a patient and supportive family who share in my foodie adventures when I can tempt them. To Vicky, Millie and Sam. Thanks you for your love and enthusiasm.

Finally, I was lucky to have grown up in an environment where good food and healthy eating were a central part of our day to day lives. There was always a home-cooked meal on the table and a fridge full of tasty leftovers so lastly I owe it all to three people, Ruth and John Winter and Margaret Maughan, aka Mum, Dad and Aunt. They are no longer around to see these stories resurrected but their spirit is buried within these pages for eternity.